By the Grace of God

A TESTIMONY OF JOHN R. AMABILE

John R. Amabile

TRILOGY CHRISTIAN PUBLISHERS
TUSTIN, CA

Trilogy Christian Publishers
A Wholly Owned Subsidiary of Trinity Broadcasting Network
2442 Michelle Drive
Tustin, CA 92780

By the Grace of God: A Testimony of John R. Amabile

Scripture quotations marked AMP are taken from the Amplified® Bible (AMP), Copyright © 2015 by The Lockman Foundation. Used by permission. www.Lockman.org.

Scripture quotations marked AMPCE are taken from the Amplified Bible, Copyright © 1954, 1958, 1962, 1964, 1965, 1987 by The Lockman Foundation. Used by permission.

Scripture quotations marked ESV are taken from the ESV® Bible (The Holy Bible, English Standard Version®), copyright © 2001 by Crossway Bibles, a publishing ministry of Good News Publishers. Used by permission. All rights reserved.

Scripture quotations marked GNT are taken from the Good News Translation® (Today's English Version, Second Edition). Copyright © 1982 American Bible Society. All rights reserved.

Scripture quotations marked NIV are taken from the Holy Bible, New International Version®, NIV®. Copyright © 1973, 1978, 1984, 2011 by Biblica, Inc.™ Used by permission of Zondervan. All rights reserved worldwide. www.zondervan.com. The "NIV" and "New International Version" are trademarks registered in the United States Patent and Trademark Office by Biblica, Inc.™

Scripture quotations marked NKJV are taken from the New King James Version®. Copyright © 1982 by Thomas Nelson. Used by permission. All rights reserved.

Scripture quotations marked (RSV) are taken from the Revised Standard Version of the Bible, copyright © 1946,1952, and 1971 National Council of the Churches of Christ in the United States of America. Used by permission. All rights reserved worldwide.

Scripture quotations marked (TLB) are taken from The Living Bible copyright © 1971. Used by permission of Tyndale House Publishers, Inc., Carol Stream, Illinois 60188. All rights reserved.

Scripture quotations marked KJV are taken from the King James Version of the Bible. Public domain.

Rights Department, 2442 Michelle Drive, Tustin, CA 92780.

Trilogy Christian Publishing/TBN and colophon are trademarks of Trinity Broadcasting Network.

For information about special discounts for bulk purchases, please contact Trilogy Christian Publishing.

Trilogy Disclaimer: The views and content expressed in this book are those of the author and may not necessarily reflect the views and doctrine of Trilogy Christian Publishing or the Trinity Broadcasting Network.

Manufactured in the United States of America

10 9 8 7 6 5 4 3 2 1

Library of Congress Cataloging-in-Publication Data is available.

ISBN: 978-1-68556-286-1

E-ISBN: 978-1-68556-287-8

Contents

Dedicated to my loving wife, Irene Amabile.

CHAPTER ONE

In the Beginning

This testimony started when I was a young boy living in the downtown section of Jersey City, New Jersey. It was the time of the depression, and very few people had jobs that paid enough for people to get along. My mother and father decided to start a business. It was a fruit and vegetable business in one section of Jersey City where people had little money. The business failed, and my father had to look for other work. We lived close to my grandmother and my grandfather, who had a very large Italian family with thirteen children. My father was one of the twelve boys. They also had one girl. My grandmother watched me for my parents while they worked.

My grandmother was a typical Italian American mother who cooked and cleaned and took care of her kids relentlessly. On Sunday, the smell of Italian meatballs and pasta made everyone in that neighborhood hungry. She baked her own bread and made her own ravioli. She also was an excellent counselor with her children. She listened and helped them with many of their problems. My grandmother was an excellent cook. Mother told me that my grandmother went to church every morning before she started her day. She attended Holy Rosary Catholic Church in Jersey City. My grandfather looked like Santa Claus; that's the only way I can explain it. He had white hair, ruddy completion, and blue eyes. He was a very handsome man who spoke broken English. He was a mason and a bricklayer. He worked every day of his life. I could hear him say on Sunday, "Johnny, come to me and give me a hug." I was the oldest male grandson he had. Both grandfathers came from the Province of Salerno, along with my mother's mother. The Amabile grandparents came from Sant'Arsenio, and the Di Geronimo grandparents came from Santa Mena, both in the Province of Salerno.

My family were not churchgoers, and I don't remember them going to church when I was a little boy, but I do remember attending classes at Holy Rosary Elementary School, which was a Catholic elementary school. I remember kneeling on the fire escape when I was bad in school. Finally, my parents took me out of that school and put me in a public school.

This took place during World War II, and my father took a job in the naval base in Kearny, New Jersey, where they were producing war ships. Everybody was concerned that when the war was over, all the veterans would come back, and many of the people who were working lost their jobs because they gave the vets first preference. People were worried about war coming to this country. It was a very patriotic time. People had victory gardens (which meant they grew their own produce); people listened to the radio every night to see how the war was going. Finally, the news broke that the war was over, and I can remember everybody jumping for joy and even getting on the back of trucks and going to various neighborhoods dancing and kissing fellow Americans. They were so happy. It was a happy time I will never forget. I was about seven years old. After the war, things changed. The ship builders and the airplane builders and the people who made ammunition all laid off their workers. My father was one of them. Everybody was happy that the war was over, but now we had a lag in the economy. My father could not find a job after the war, and he looked in Connecticut for work.

Finances were tough at the time, and I was only a little boy. I mean, I wasn't aware of what was going on, but I knew that they had to move from that location to another location because my father looked for a different job from what he was doing. So he took a job as a lineman in Connecticut, and he traveled up to Connecticut on Sunday and then came back by Friday. We would have him for two days a week. We really didn't have a family that was working. My story really begins on the last day of school in 1947. I could remember being very happy that school was over for two months and I was on vacation. I came home, and my mother was bathing my sister. The radio playing was a very nice setting for the last day of school and my father coming home from Connecticut. I was very happy, but around half past three in the afternoon, there was a knock on the door, and there were two men in suits who wanted to speak to my mother. I called my mother and told her that there were two men at the door and they wanted to speak to her. So she answered the door, and I went to take care of the baby. Then, I heard a scream that I will never forget. My father was working on high wire lines for the railroad and had an accident; he was killed on the high wires. This was devastating not only to my mother but to the whole family. The question they were all asking was how they could help in this situation. My mother's brothers and her younger sister decided that they would pool finances, and we would have one dinner meal together as a family. This was a blessing for my brother and sister and me. I will explain in a few parts of the testimony how they helped us more than one time.

I decided to help, so I made a shoeshine box and shone shoes in two of the taverns. I also had a paper route and made at least ten to twelve dollars a week.

BY THE GRACE OF GOD

One of the positive experiences I had at Our Lady of Mt. Carmel was the novenas with the Jesuit priests. They would come in and say novenas, and many of them were really great teachers. This gave me a good sampling of what life would be like as a Christian. I heard the gospels, but I can't say that I remember too much. I only know it had an influence on the beginning of my walk with God. I just know that I felt secure, if you could at that age.

My uncle and aunt helped us get a three-family house, so that was income for my mom and my brother, sister, and me, and we had a house where we had a roof over our head. My uncle Mike helped with the down payment, so we were able to have a nice house with an income. This was a miracle in itself; we were so happy. The house needed a lot of work, so I called my friend Joe Lauro who was on the football team with me and was working in a wood mill company. He knew how to fix windows and even helped make kitchen cabinets for my mother. My brother and I were not the best workers, but with the help of Joe, we got the job done.

This was good preparation for later in life when we both had our own home.

Moving into this new area meant I had to go to a new school. This made a big difference in my life: new kids, new teachers, and a new start. Mr. Kaplan, the physical education teacher, took a liking to me. He was also in charge of the crossing guards. In those days, they had crossing guards that were children, and the head guy was my friend Ralph, who became a lifelong friend. Ralph was a sports enthusiast. He liked baseball and all sports games, and I did too, so we got along very well. He moved up and became the captain of the crossing guards, and then he moved on to play football at the high school. I took his place as the school crossing guard captain.

The school was much more welcoming than the other schools I attended. I needed this change. It really helped me, as I felt like I had a place here, and I did very well in class. I liked the teachers; the teachers liked me. It wasn't just a good experience; I knew that I would be going to high school and probably seeing and playing ball with Ralph. At that point, there wasn't much growth spiritually. I went to church on Sunday and many times stopped in church on the way to school. I was able to do that because we walked to school.

I had a great time in high school playing football, and as a result, I had a lot of friends. I went to two proms, had a girlfriend, but I did little schoolwork to help myself get to some of the goals I had. By this time, my mother had a job working at RCA in Harrison, New Jersey, and she had to work nights, so our family life was really interrupted. It was just me, my sister, and my brother. So schoolwork and reading weren't getting done. These were the things I needed to do to prepare myself for life.

One time my uncle had a stroke, so I took over for him while I went to high school. It was a great experience taking over a business for my uncle so he would not lose any business, and thank God for that. There were many cold, snowy nights that I was out delivering oil to those who needed it for heat. The streets in the city were very narrow, and it was so hard to drive and double park the truck in the street. Then, I would take the hose from the truck and run with it so it picked up momentum. That way, the hose moved very easily. Sometimes I was out there until ten o'clock in the evening delivering, and I had to go to school the next day. This was hard, but it gave me the drive to be responsible and appreciate what it was to have a job and have other people rely on you.

Now it was time for me to meet with my counselor and decide on plans for the future. I had so many interruptions in my life. At that age, it was so hard to sit and decide on a plan for my life. When I met with my counselor, she said to be prepared to work on construction or do some kind of other work. I told her I wanted to go to college, and she told me that it was not in the future for me.

While this was taking place, a teacher, Winnifred Sullivan, who had taken a liking to me, made a difference. As I look back at my life, God had His hand on people in my life to be there when I had a decision to make. Miss Sullivan called me outside her class one day and said to me, "It's all over." I said, "What's all over?" She said, "Coming to school and not working. You are going to work in this class, or you are not going to graduate." Between the counselor and Miss Sullivan, I got the message. As I look back, I can see how the Lord was giving me the message, but at the time, I didn't realize it. I had to produce. I had to do something in school that was going to get me to the next level.

There was another time I had a job in construction, working seven days a week. Working seven days a week was a lot of money, so my uncle said, "Why don't you drop out of school and at least finish the job?" This was working on the Newark by extension of the New Jersey Turnpike. I dropped out of school, but I went to an evening school, taking the same courses I needed. My uncle told me that he would save the money for me so we could pay off my uncle, who put up the down payment for the house. I did that, and everybody was happy. I thank God that I was able to help my mom.

St. Benedict's/Northwest Missouri State College

My friend George Tardiff, who played next to me on the line at Lincoln High, called me and said, "John, how are you doing with your quest for college?" I told him I enrolled in Seton Hall University in a satellite location in Jersey City. George was asking about a football scholarship.

George said to me, "We tried everything else; why don't we try God?" I said, "What do you mean?" He said, "We can go to a little church in Jersey City to a novena."

When I was an altar boy at Our Lady of Mount Carmel Church many years ago, I attended many novenas, so I was okay with that. So George and I went on a mission to try God on our quest for college. We went to a little church in Jersey City. We did that for about four weeks, and one night, George gave me a call and said that a friend called him from St. Benedict's and said the coach would like to see him, so he packed his bags and went out to Atchison, Kansas.

George said to me, "When I get out there, I will tell the coach about you; then, you can come out." George was about six foot three, about 240-pounds, a Norwegian-looking guy with blue eyes and blond hair and just a nice guy.

What faith these two guys had in me to tell their coach about me. George went out in January, and I got a call from George in May. This was God's favor, and what a miracle. "I told you I would call you. The coach would like to see you, so pack your bags." Bill Turka was the guy that called George. George and I bought a car, a 1948 Pontiac, that only had two gears. Now my journey out west and a taste of God's favor were on me. This was a faith walk, not knowing the coach and the area, only going by what George and Bill told me. It was a Catholic all-boys school and had a great football team. The school had a good reputation. They told me all about Coach Shotell and the school. It seemed too good to be true. I was now going from Jersey to Atchison, Kansas, on a word of faith!

Scripture influence
Matthew 7:9–11 (KJV):

> Or what man is there of you, whom if his son ask bread, will he give him a stone? Or if he ask a fish, will he give him a serpent? If ye then, being evil, know how to give good gifts unto your children, how much more shall your Father which is in heaven give good things to them that ask him?

When my father died in 1947, it was a very sad day for our entire family. We were without a breadwinner of the house and a strong leader for our family. We quickly became very insecure. God's love touched my uncles and my aunt, and they provided the security we needed. My uncles took me to the church and introduced me to the priest at church, and the church gave me the spiritual support I needed at the time.

I got security from the family, who not only supported us with their presence but also monetarily. They helped buy food and kept the house going. When my uncles involved me in the church, I just knew God was there for me. I don't know how I knew, but in my spirit, I just knew. This accordance happened throughout my life. One of the big blessings of God's favor was when we were able to buy a house with the help of my uncles. What a blessing they were. Prior to this event, I devoted my time to the church, assisting in masses and anything they needed in the church. I felt the loss of my father, but I did feel God's love in the people at the church.

I don't remember asking for help, and I did not realize the growth in our relationship until the future. What I have tried to capture in this book is the favor God had on my life. Maybe a young person could see hope in their life through my experiences, which looked hopeless and turned out to be a very successful life spiritually and in my profession. I had miracle after miracle. When I looked back, I could see God's favor though out my life. It wasn't until I met Jesus that all this made sense. It will be explained in later chapters. I did not realize the voice on my inside, which many times was not vocal, was God speaking to me. Many decisions in the future were made with that tug in my heart and not knowing God had it under control.

"Do not be seized with alarm and struck with fear, little flock, for it is you father's desire to give you the kingdom" (Luke 12:32, AMPC).

When we moved to the new house with the help of my uncles and aunt, what a blessing; God put people in our life to take away the fear and show us His kingdom. Mr. Kaplan, the gym teacher who made me feel very important and gave me the job of captain of the crossing guards, did so much for me. Imagine what a blessing. Ralph, as a friend, was in my life like a big brother at the time I needed him. Winifred Sullivan was there to support me in high school and gave me the help and the courage to write in the yearbook at the high school. He gave me His kingdom by placing the right people in my life at the right time.

Psalm 68:5 (AMP), "...father of the Fatherless and protector of widows is God in his holy habitation."

This is another scripture that states how God is the Father of the fatherless. It is my belief that this was the tug I felt in my gut to make the right decision. God surrounded me with good people, my uncles, the priests at our Lady of Mount Carmel Church to help me make the right decisions in life at this time. The big city had many good influences, but it also had some bad ones. Thank God I had the influence to make the right decisions and had the family I had and the career.

CHAPTER TWO

Atchison, Kansas

When we got to Atchison, we went right to the school. The campus was beautiful. Coming from Jersey City and not going too far from the city, I was impressed. We went to the gym where the coach had his office, and everything was clean and well cared for. George and Bill took me to see Coach Shotell. They introduced me to the coach, and his first words were, "Are you good?" I said, "Do you think I would come halfway across this country if I wasn't good?" We had a good laugh, and he said, "I like you, boy." The coach told me to get my transcript and was going to go talk to the priest. We sat and waited and talked about the school and what would be my major. I told everybody I would like to be a football coach and major in business education and physical education.

The coach came back, and he said the priest said he could not give me a scholarship. The coach said if I attended a school in Missouri where his college coach was still coaching, I could transfer and get the scholarship (God's favor). He wanted to know if I would do that, and I said, "Yes." He called a boy who went to that school, and he drove me up there. His name was Jim Taylor. We drove up the next day and looked for the coach, who was Ryland Milner. The coach had called him and made all the arrangements with the other coach. What I did not realize was that he was giving me a scholarship at this school. I did not realize at the time I had a scholarship to Northwest Missouri, and if I wanted to stay there, I could. I was so happy I had to pinch myself at God putting this all together.

Going to school was a big adjustment for me. I was playing football and had fraternity involvement and schoolwork, so it was very hard. Jim became my roommate, and he was really a nice person who invited me to his home, and I met his whole family. I had never been to the Midwest, so I was very impressed with the hospitality. Jim and I are lifelong friends. I still see him at least once a year.

When I looked at the size of the football players on this team, I was kind of small, but I was going to give it the best of my ability. It was a struggle keeping up with my grades, football, and everything. During the football season, I got hurt again on my knee and had to lay in the back of the bus from Doane University to Maryville, Missouri. I was in pain the whole trip back home.

The name of my college was Northwest Missouri State College, and it was about a four-hour ride to Doan.

I felt every bump on the road. The next day, I was told to go to the school doctor, and he told me he thought I needed an operation on the knee. I was not about to get another operation. I tried to heal naturally, and I did not heal. I could not play football, but what I did not realize was that I could not play at college with this kind of injury.

This year was okay with finances, but the year coming up, I would have to pay. I came home that year and worked on construction and went back in the fall. My grades were much better not having football and not being involved in the fraternity. I ran out of money that semester and decided I would come home, work, and come back the following September.

I found a student who lived in New York and was going to my school, so I made arrangements with him to come home. When I got home, my mother was so happy to see me. She told me that my friends had invited me to go to a dance. She gave me money for the dance ticket, so I went to the dance with them.

I walked to the Fairmount Hotel, which was about four or five blocks from where I lived. I borrowed two dollars from my mother for transportation to the dance because I didn't have money, and otherwise, I would have to walk home.

The dance was on the roof of the hotel in their ballroom. I bought the ticket and went to step into the elevator, and there was a girl standing also waiting to get on the elevator, so I let her go first. She was a beautiful blonde with a red dress, and she made me nervous. We were the only two in the elevator. She put out her hand and said, "Hi, I am Irene Yankers. What's your name?" I said, "John Amabile." "Are you the John Amabile!" I said, "Yes, I am." She was thinking of my cousin by the same name that played quarterback for Boston College. We both played football at the same time in the city, so people got confused about who was who. I did not let her go.

We danced every dance, and we both danced the same moves. We had a great time. *Now how do I get her home? I don't have a car, and I don't have any money.* My cousin Lorraine was at the dance, so I asked her if I could use her car to take this new date home. My cousin Lorraine said, "You better be careful; this car is new. My father would kill both of us if anything happened to that car." This is the daughter of the uncle who owned the oil company. Lorraine was my age, and we were very close growing up. She graduated from Snyder High, the rival of Lincoln High, where I went to school.

This was when I met Irene, who would be my wife for fifty-nine years. She was the prettiest girl at the dance, and we were flying high. From that point on, I saw Irene every day, and we started to plan a future.

This was one of the big miracles in my life because this girl became the mother of my children. God's favor was on me. I just knew this was the right girl.

Scripture influence

Second Corinthians 12:9, "'My grace is sufficient for thee: for my strength is made perfect in weakness.' Most gladly therefore will I rather glory in my infirmities, that the power of Christ may rest upon me."

Just the idea to go that far from home based on a phone call from a friend who went to church with you to get a scholarship to go to college. This is the weak made strong. The hand of God was on the two of us. George, getting a scholarship to St. Benedict's, and me, receiving one from Northwest Missouri State College. There is no question that this was not a move in our strength but in our heart. We turned to God as a last resort, and He came through for us big time. The situation was made perfect in our weakness. This is one of the key points for me in writing this book. There is hope in relying on the power of God! This was the beginning of my walk. I knew something happened I did not totally understand. I understand now when I look back at my life that there was favor all along the way. The problem was I did not recognize it until I had a relationship with Jesus, which happened later in my life. I could feel the love and care from the coach and the priest who reviewed my application. When I look back at this miracle, I see God's hand because what he had for me later blew my mind. Just review these points: (1) I went across the country on blind faith, (2) had fair preparation for college, and (3) got to go to college. This is what you call a miracle!

Ephesians 2 (KJV), "For by grace are ye saved though faith: and that not of by us: it is the gift of God: not of works, lest any man should boast."

I may have been saved, but I was making the mistakes the world makes. I did not hold up to the side of the bargain, and I started to slip in my grades and with the money I had to continue. What followed was very hard academically and socially; I was not used to a fraternity. It was hard, with too much interference in what I was there for. Without proper guidance, I slipped. I decided to go home and work and make money and come back and finish up. When I look back at this part of my life, what are the chances that I would come back? I think a slim chance. I came home on a Saturday, and my friends were going to a dance on Sunday. I did not have a car or money, so I borrowed money from my mother to go to the dance. When I got there, I purchased a ticket and proceeded to get on the elevator when a pretty girl got on before me. When we got on the elevator, she put out her hand and said, "Hi, I am Irene Yankers. What is your name?" This was another miracle in my life; this was the girl I would marry, have three children and five grandchildren with. Not only was she good-looking, but she was also a sweetheart. We got married, and we went back, and I finished my degree. What are the chances of flying home on Saturday and on Sunday meeting the person you would spend the rest of your life with? We were married for fifty-nine years and had a wonderful life with ups and downs, but our love got us through it all. I was really motivated to get my degree and get life started. We were happy to be married, and my mother was so happy that day.

Ephesians 1:7–10 (KJV):

> In whom we have redemption through his blood, the forgiveness of sins, according to his riches of his grace: wherein he hath abounded toward us in all wisdom and prudence; having made known unto us the mystery of his will according to his good pleasure which he hath purpose in himself that in the dispensation of the fulness of times he might gather together in one all things in Christ, both which are in heaven and which are on earth; even in him.

We are sinners saved by grace; at the time, I did not know or understand the forgiveness of God. He had forgiven all my sins before I confessed how sorry I was.

He had given me such a gift, and I let it go because of worldly interference. But I did know that I was getting another chance, and I was not going to mess it up. College made a lot more sense to me being married. We were there for about a year and a half, and Irene was pregnant and went home before I did.

CHAPTER THREE

We Were Married 8/8/1959

Now Irene and I were married on August 8, 1959. We didn't go on a long honeymoon because we were going to move back to Maryville, Missouri, and go to college at Northwest Missouri State. We decided to go to Wildwood, New Jersey, for a honeymoon. It was a nice long weekend, and it was a very loving relationship, and I'll never forget that. We came home and visited with family because we were leaving to go to Maryville, Missouri, in another week. Irene was a little apprehensive about going back to Missouri because she had a good job in New York City, and she really didn't want to leave that. Anyway, we were back to visit family and friends, and it was very nice for us to see them, but it was heart-wrenching because we knew that we were going to be away from them for a long time. I bought a car from my uncle, a '49 Studebaker. I hoped it would get us across the country to Maryville.

I had already arranged to see an apartment that was in downtown Maryville. The apartment was over a typewriter store, and it had a blinking light that lit up the whole apartment when it went on. My friends thought this was a funny part of this apartment on and off lights. When we got to the apartment, it was dark out, so you could not see the bed or anything in the apartment. When we woke up the next morning, Irene noticed the wallpaper in the kitchen had cows on it. That didn't go over too well with her. Then there was a cattle truck under our bedroom window; all you could hear was "Mooooo." She was not too happy.

Maryville was a quaint town with a town center and a city hall in the middle. As you rode down the main drive to the college, there were all pretty old midwestern houses. Pulling up to the college were these big pine trees that were just beautiful. I must say it was a great place to go to school. The people in this town were very hospitable, much different than the people who lived in Jersey City. We had some friends, Ed and Marsha, with whom we shared many meals. Ed went on to be a football coach for a school in Kansas. Bob Severson and Zoe Anne were two people who were close to Irene and me. Bob wanted me to sing at their church, the Presbyterian Church, and I did. I sang "I Love You Truly." Bob went on to be a very successful farmer in the area. Zoe Anne was a great golfer. The campus was the traditional administration building with the look of the Ivory Towers. It was just a great campus and a great place to go to school. This is the place where I should mention that in the last ten years, they were national champs in football three times.

The homecoming at this school was a big deal. All the organizations in the towns from Iowa and Missouri participate in this big event. I have never seen a bigger event than homecoming at Northwest Missouri State College. My friends Jim Taylor, Jack Little, and Bob Severson were master of ceremonies at homecoming. We were called the four Ivys.

We were living in Maryville, which was about two miles from the campus I have just described. There were very few jobs available in Maryville, and Irene was having a hard time finding one. We had an advantage: we found out that she could receive unemployment insurance for a short period of time until she could find a job. Things were going very well in school. She was not liking living in Missouri, but we made a commitment, so she was going to find a job in Maryville.

It was Christmas time, and we thought that we would come back home. Irene wanted to see her family. When we decided to come home, she lost her unemployment. Now, we would not have any money when we came back to school. We both would have to work to support the two of us. So we continued for about two or three months. The landlord wanted to be paid his rent, but we couldn't make the payments. We went to see Mr. Patterson to see if he would go along with us in terms of making payments. I told him that if he wanted us to leave, he just had to say the word, and we would leave. He told us as long as I was getting my degree, I could stay in the apartment until I could pay him back. Irene and I both were so touched by this man's attitude. I will never forget this man had millions.

I got a gig (job) singing in a local band; they heard me sing at homecoming, and they wanted me to sing with them. We needed the money, so whatever I could do, I did to support us. I also had a job cleaning a laundromat. I would go there once a day and make sure it was clean. That paid about $40.00 a month; that paid for our food. I also worked at Cornet Chevy in Maryville, cleaning the showroom. Meanwhile, Irene got a job in the Yells Music Shop in town. We were supporting ourselves and learned many good lessons in survival. The Lord took care of our place to live and food on our table.

My coursework was almost finished, and it was time to graduate and go home to get a job. Irene was now pregnant with our daughter Irene. Irene flew home about three months before she gave birth.

Now it was time for me to see Dr. Foster, dean of the college, to see if I had all the credits to graduate. He had told me that for me to graduate, I would have to get straight As my last semester. I knew that because I had a record of what courses I had and what I needed. Now that time had come: all courses were finished, and everybody was going home. I went in to see Dr. Foster. He told me he could not tell me if I graduated because grades were not in. He told me to call him from the airport, and he would tell me.

First thing at the airport, I called Dr. Foster, and he told me I had fifteen credits of As and I would graduate. I was so happy; I felt like the weight of the world was off my shoulders. When I got home, my mother had a party for me; she was so proud. All my friends were invited. My mother even made room for us to dance. Maryville was a nice place to go to school, but it was so nice to be home. The next morning, Irene went through labor. This was the day my daughter was born, at three fifteen in the afternoon. What a powerful weekend. Now, I was blessed with a family!

I had all the tools I needed to pursue my dream, which was to teach and coach. I applied and got a job teaching business in the school from which I graduated, Lincoln High School. My cousin by the same name (John N. Amabile) played at Boston College and took a head coaching job in that school. Do you remember Ralph? He was also one of the coaching staff.

This was a great experience working with John. I learned a lot about football, which would come in handy in my next job. John N. (as he was called) played quarterback for Boston College and had an excellent experience, so it was all good working with him. Ralph and I had the same job teaching business and coaching football. Another opportunity came our way to teach in an adult education course at Dickerson High in Jersey City.

We both had the same family goal, and that was to buy a house in the suburb to bring up our children in a home like we never had. Now we had two children. Karen, my second child, was born when we lived in Jersey City.

After three years of successful teaching, we decided to look for a job in south Jersey.

Ralph took a job in Matawan, and I took a job in Jackson, New Jersey. My career skyrocketed. It was like the Lord was waiting to make a move to bless me. I was in Jackson for one year, and I became chairman of the business department. It was the first year of school, and many traditions had to be started. After that next year, the vice-principal asked me if I would like to be an assistant. There was one assistant, but they wanted another. I told him I was not certified to do that. He said he would call the county and get six months for me to get the credits. I took four courses in four different schools and received the certification.

Then the football team was losing all their games and the athletic director, Don Connor, asked me if I would like to be the head coach of the football team. My dream job! I said yes, and I coached football and was assistant principal at the same time. Now the school was getting crowded, and we went to double session. This was a challenge.

Coaching football was a desire of my heart. I loved the job and loved the kids on the team. It was a struggle coaching these kids, as they were in Lakewood before coming to Jackson. That was one problem; the other problem was the school was growing so fast that every year, we were moving up to another class, never really having success at any level. I always said that they should have kept us on one level until we matured in the league. All in all, I loved those kids and tried very hard to have a winning season, but it never happened. The thing that I cherish is the friendship of the boys I coached. I still hear from them, and they are all successful people.

You get to teach many life skills coaching, and it is a daily challenge. You actually become another parent helping them get through the problems in life in the school setting. I could see my career moving in another direction. I was getting that nag again, and I knew it was time to move on. I also became dear friends with the other coaches that were going through this. People like Larry and Carol D'Zio, with whom I have remained friends since 1964. It's almost like family because of the problem we had to solve getting a new school started. Greg Mick, Gus Christ, and John Kovack are all students that I am in touch with on Facebook.

Middle States Evaluation

The Middle States Evaluation is a certification group that comes to visit a school district to see if they are doing what they proposed in the district objective. Students in this district would not get the chance to go to college if their district did not have the certification. This was a big thing for our district, and I had little experience in doing this big job.

When we came off double session, we were ready for the Middle States Evaluation. This happens to new schools so they can get certified.

With all the challenges the superintendent gave me, I did them well. He now called me into his office and told me he wanted me to be chairman of the middle states committee. I told him I did not have experience in that process, and he told me he knew I would do a good job. One of the problems was that this was a new school, and they did not have a course outline, and it was needed for this evaluation.

I went back to my old high school and met with Dr. Losi (Dr. Losi was my high school principal, and when I taught in Lincoln, he was my boss), and he said I could have a copy of their course outline as a model. Dr. Losi was thrilled that I came back to see him and asked for help. I took the outlines and spoke to my committee and told them what I wanted them to do. He told me he was on a few evaluations, so he knew exactly what I needed. What a blessing! In six months of working after school, they developed the outline, and we were ready for the evaluation. There were about forty people who came from many different states to do this. Many principals and college professors did the evaluation.

Jackson Memorial High

The staff at the high school was very cooperative; we could not have accomplished this without the professionalism of this staff. I was so proud of the teachers at Jackson Memorial High School. We passed this evaluation with flying colors thanks to those teachers who were teaching in the school at the time. To get me ready for the next my next position, the superintendent transferred me to the middle school. We had a dinner meeting, and they presented us with the knowledge that we passed the evaluation with flying colors. The board of education was very satisfied with the certification.

The next school built in Jackson would be a middle school, and the money was presented to us from the state. The board of education wanted to try a new school because the next school to be built was going to be a middle school. The principal of the present middle school was Gerry Riley, who was the professor who taught the first college class I took at Seton Hall in Jersey City. You think this was a coincidence? I don't think so. When I was appointed, Gerry and I had a good laugh; after all these years, we were back together.

I worked one year at the Clayton Middle School, getting ready for the new school. There was one incident the Lord used me for in this school. Looking back, I remember there was a boy who was killed in the school with one of those doors that divide the gym between boys and girls. The boys got the key and were playing chicken, and one got caught. Two teachers will always be my heroes, George Deader and Marty Silverman. They gave mouth-to-mouth resuscitation from the school to the hospital, which was about twenty minutes away, and I witnessed this whole incident. I never told them, but I will tell them now they are my heroes.

Paterson Road School (Goetz Middle School) and New School Paterson Road School (Goetz Middle School)

The school built in Jackson would be a middle school, and the money was presented to us from the state. The board of education wanted to try a new system of education, which was the open school. I told the superintendent that I did not have experience in doing this kind of education and that if he wanted me to do this, he would have to send me to visit other schools. So I visited other schools to see what open school was like, and I came back to him and reported that I was very impressed with the quality of education and enthusiasm of the teachers and the principal. I told him that this was something that I would like to do, so we proceeded to look at plans for a new school and for me to visit other schools in the area and out of the area that had this kind of a concept; we developed the curriculum. Some parents liked it; some parents did not like it. It was working very well; students were all reading above the level and were above the level in math. I had the teachers work on much of the curriculum, and I supported them one hundred percent. They would work after school putting this school together, and I had to sometimes tell them they had to leave. You would not believe the enthusiasm. The Lord laid on my heart that I was to create a school that was *encouraging to teachers*. In other words, I had to fertilize the atmosphere and make it positive and encouraging. With this attitude, teachers would grow as well as students. Teachers wanted to use this motto for the school, "They treat us like people." I don't know if that would work today, but it did work at the time. One of the problems with the school was that the parents wanted teachers standing in front of the class. At this school, we had large group instruction, small group instruction, and individualization; we tested students every week to put them on their level. This was prescriptive teaching, giving them exactly what they needed to improve their skills.

A big problem developed. I found myself defending this school to teachers in other schools and parents and the board of education. They called the state for some help, and they came in and were so impressed with this kind of set that they gave me a part-time job at Monmouth College teaching graduate teachers some of the methods we used in this school. Parents and the board were not impressed. At that time, the superintendent left for another job, and they moved me to another school, and that was the end of the program. Looking back, one of the problems with me personally was this was my baby, and I was proud of this. When we have too much pride in anything, there is always a fall, and for me, this was a fall.

There are so many things I could tell you that were cutting edge in education. I was so proud of the teachers and staff for the job they did. I am going to list some of the things we did so you can get a flavor for the atmosphere in this school. This school became the Goetz Middle School in Jackson, New Jersey.

1.   I tried to create a happy atmosphere and talked to the teachers about having a positive attitude.

2. We had a term we used: "Killer statements." These were put-downs that students were not allowed to use because they hurt other students. Teachers had lessons about how it felt when somebody put you down. Parents loved this program; teachers were required to have class meetings once a day to talk about these problems.

3. Greeting all the parents and teachers with a smile would be an unwritten thing we would do.

4. Reading and math were individualized so that students would not be frustrated and were learning at their own level.

5. Teachers were totally involved in the planning of either curriculum or programs to build self-image.

6. As a principal, I tried to get around to each class at least twice a week.

7. Teacher evaluations were based on improving instruction. In Jackson, we had many programs that we wanted to have teachers use in classrooms, and it was my job to see these being used. I evaluated how well the teacher used these techniques.

8. We had a club program that encouraged teachers to do their hobbies in school as a club. It was great for teacher morale.

There were so many good ideas in this school, too many to mention in a book like this. If I was to evaluate this program, I would give it an A-plus for the simple reason that the teachers cared, and they wanted to improve too. We have had meetings just on how we can improve on what we do.

The biggest problem was the program started in the middle and not in the entire school district. You can't have one grade doing one thing and other grades doing other things. Curriculum is sequential. What happened to the school? The administration moved principals around and shut down the program.

CHAPTER FOUR

Johnson Elementary School

I was moved to the elementary school, but I am going to stop here for another thing that happened in my life.

Irene's girlfriend called her and said she was going to a marriage encounter and would like to know if we wanted to go. I was sponsored by Saint Joseph Church in Toms River, the church we attended at the time. We went and had a great experience. We were touched by it, and we both fell in love over again. Then, this same girl was going to a Catholic charismatic prayer meeting at the church. We agreed to go and were very impressed with the meeting.

I told my wife they were doing something in the back room and I would like to see what was going on. The leader of this group was a superintendent in the Berkeley Township School District, so I wanted to see what was going on. We went to the following meeting, and after the meeting, I went to the back room, which was a chapel.

I opened the door, looked in, and saw a nun sitting in a chair, having people pray for her. When I opened the door, they instructed me to come in. I said, "What for?" and they said, "We will pray for you." I said, "I don't need prayer; I just wanted to see what was going on." The nun said she was finished, and I could sit. One fellow was Roy, and he was the one who wanted me to sit, so I did. I have never been the same since. They laid hands on me, and it was like the Father was saying to me, "I have been with you all these years; now, you know I love you." I filled up with tears and started crying, and they prayed and praised the Lord, and I did too.

He Touched Me

I knew He touched me, and something happened in my life. *How do I explain to my wife what happened?* I did not have to, as she grabbed and held me as if she knew. I had a problem handling the school situation, and we had money problems, but now life was good for other reasons. Sal Graziano was also in that group, and Sal was the music minister, so I told Sal I would like to play with him at the prayer meeting. He asked me, "Do you play?" and I said, "No, can you teach me?" He smiled and said yes. This started a long relationship with Sal that I will explain. Joan Smith also wanted to sing with us at the prayer meeting, and we formed a singing group called By the Grace of God.

While this was happening, things were happening in my job as a principal. It was no longer a job; it was my ministry. Now, when I went to school each day, I felt that I had an obligation to children, teachers, and parents. It was a caring atmosphere. What the Lord put in my heart was very simple. If I was encouraging teachers, they would encourage their students. This proved to be very helpful throughout the school from this point. In the Johnson School, with the help of the music teacher, we had an assembly with the children to sing Christmas carols, and I played the guitar, and he played the piano. He was a blessing for the children and for me. I asked the music teacher if he would like our group, By the Grace of God, to play at his sing-along at the Jewish Community Center. He asked, "What would you sing?" I told him we had Old Testament songs that we could do. He told me to give him the songs, and I did. The rabbi said it was fine. We were very excited to do this, so we showed up at the Beth Israel Temple in Lakewood to sing for a group of about twenty-five people. At first, they were apprehensive, but as we sang and played, they loosened up. Our last song was "Halva Nigella," and we brought the house down. They were all dancing and very happy. They could not give us enough cheesecake.

Maria

I started to reach out to all students and teachers. There was a girl named Maria who was a special little girl who had very special needs. Her brother knew my son in school, so we asked if I could go to her house and minister in song to her. It made it easier because my son knew the brother. I asked the mother if she would like me to come over and play my guitar for her at least once a week. Her mother was thrilled that I would do that; she said yes, and I went. Last Christmas, my son heard from her brother; he wanted to thank me for taking the time for his sister. That was at least thirty years ago.

Parenting

I was in a doctoral program and developed a program in parenting. I researched and put this program together for parents. We met in the evening to go over the program but also to talk to each other about what they were doing with their children. Parents loved this program. The point is that with the Lord in my life, I was trying to help parents and children. I felt responsible for getting them as much information as possible. I knew that education starts with the parents. If they were in tune, the children would also be. The underlying factor was now, with the Lord in my life, I had to do the best I could. I represented Him, and He wanted the best for His children.

So many things happened now that I knew the Lord. There was that nudging that I had a long time ago to share the Lord with other people. One day, my supervisor called me in to talk to me about something, so I went to see her. When I was finished, I went to my car, but before I got there, something inside me told me to invite this supervisor to the Full Gospel meeting at Tommy's restaurant. I was going to pay for the meal, so it was not a hard-to-accept invite. I turned around and went back in the school and invited this lady to the meeting, and she was delighted.

At the Meeting

At the meeting, there was a presentation, and at the end of the meeting, an altar call. The supervisor got up and took the altar call. We were both so happy; I gave her a big hug! She told me she invited someone to the meeting, and that person not only got saved but also started his own church. This lady's name was Mary, and she was a no-nonsense kind of person. She told me that she had accepted the Lord long ago, and this was her coming back to Him. I was so happy.

When I look at the problems I had and I compare them to the grace and favor that God gave me, they are no match. So many of the problems I had faded, and I was on board to do what He wanted me to do.

Humorous Story

One day, I drove my convertible Triumph to school. It was a nice sunny spring day, and I thought it was a good idea. When the bell rang at 3 p.m., I saw a little boy sitting in my office. I asked my secretary why he was there, and she told me she could not get ahold of his mother to pick him up. We waited until 4 p.m., and the mother still was not home. So I told the secretary that I would drive him home. We walked out in front of the building, and his eyes lit up when he saw the car, a little Kelly-green convertible Triumph. It was beautiful. So we got in the car, and he had a big smile on his face, and I started to drive away. I must tell you the home was in a development not far from the school. We were driving in the development, and some of the kids in the development saw me driving this boy home. They all started to run and follow the little car. I was like the pied piper. All in all, when I got to the boy's house, there were about twenty kids all happy. They wanted me to take them for a ride.

Scripture Influence

1. First Peter 1:22 (NIV), "Now that you have purified yourselves by obeying the truth so that you have sincere love for each other, love one another deeply, from the heart."

Irene and I loved each other deeply from the heart, so it was an easy decision to go across the country, but in action, it was hard. The reason that we could do this was because of our love for each other. We made a commitment to love each other till death do us part, and that was what we did. Looking back at this time in life, I wouldn't want it any other way. It was a struggle for money and just being away from family. We both grew from this experience; we could make it on our own. We set goals and achieved them and even had a baby for a graduation gift. God's hand was on this move. It was a struggle, but it really paid off. This was a blessing; that was the favor of God on our lives. This struggle and achievement was a lesson and a sign in our lives that God was with us.

2. Romans 12:8 (NIV), "...if it is to encourage, then give encouragement; if it is giving, then give generously; if it is to lead, do it diligently; if it is to show mercy, do it cheerfully."

When Mr. Patterson allowed us to remain in the apartment, that definitely was God's favor. All he had to do was say he did not want to go along with the plan, and we would have gone home. We told him we would pay him, but we could not right now. He told us to stay in the apartment until we got our degrees, and then we could pay him back. He was an angel, and we appreciated him so much. He was a man who had all the money you could have, and he was being generous with us and did it cheerfully. We both said what a good man this was, and maybe someday we could do this for someone else.

3. Hebrews 11:1 (KJV), "Now faith is the substance of things hoped for, the evidence of things not seen."

Irene went back home; she was pregnant. The fraternity offered me a room in their house until graduation. I had faith that I would graduate, but I also knew I had to work for straight As; you don't just pray; you must work along with having faith. I learned a big lesson, and I was not going to let this opportunity pass by again. I worked hard. I was hoping and working for the evidence I did not see. Straight As last semester equals graduation. The boys in the fraternity house took care of me like I was family, and I have a place in my heart for these boys.

4. First Corinthians 2:5 (KJV), "That your faith should not stand on the wisdom of men but in the power of God."

God gave me the intelligence and the courage to work hard and not give up, and I did that. It was through His power that I succeeded. When I made the phone call to Dr. Forster and he told me I had reached my goal, I could feel a rush and tears of happiness in my eyes. There is nothing like God's grace when working toward a goal. I was up on the mountain; I could see, by faith, this was the start of my career. When I look back at it, I thank Him every day for what He has done for me with a wonderful past and a great future. I don't think God is through with me yet. I have a strong gut feeling that I will be around for a while. Only with God at the age of eighty-six can you start a new career. He has blessed me by faith, and He wants me to bless other people. Praise God!

5. Acts 20:24 (KJV), "But none of these things move me, neither count I my life dear unto myself that I might finish my course with joy, and the ministry, which I have received on to the Lord Jesus, to testify the gospel of the grace of God."

Now I had tools to start teaching and being a football coach. What I did not understand was what God wanted me for was a bigger game in life. He wanted me to work with children and create a climate of learning in public schools and encourage parents, teachers, and students. He gave me the insight that they all had to be in harmony with one another. He also was very clear in my later years that I had to be a sample of the gospel. I am a sinner saved by grace, but I had obligations to put the gospel out there sometimes by witnessing but most of the time through my actions.

6. John 3:16 (NIV), "...God loved the world so much that he gave his one son and only Son so that whoever believes in him may not be lost but have eternal life."

All Christians have a duty to share the gospel and to tell the world that if they believe, they will have eternal life. I felt the urge to invite the supervisor to the Full Gospel meeting so that she could meet Jesus. Little did I know that she had fallen away, and He was reaching out for her. That night at Tommy's restaurant, He did, and she responded. We became very good friends and shared the gospel with each other. If I had not invited her to the meeting, who knows what would have happened to her. PS: I also saw a change in her attitude, and that was good.

CHAPTER FIVE

The Holman
Elementary School

The Holman Elementary School

The board had another rotation of principals in the district, and I was moved again to the Holman Elementary School. I was very apprehensive because this school had a reputation of being very supportive of the teacher's union. They had many grievances that came from this school; this was going to be a challenge for me. Like anything else, we deal with what God has His hand in decisions like this, and there is always a reason. All in all, this had to be one of the most pleasurable experiences in my career. I knew in this school I had to use all the skills I had to win them over. I tried to give them personal attention and was seriously interested in the children in their class. We had an excessive number of teachers who thought many of the children in their classes were special education. I was overwhelmed with the number of referrals that were coming into the team that evaluated the referrals. I decided that I would form a committee to help teachers with the students in their class. I would meet with them every Monday morning with ten or twelve teachers, and we would listen to the teacher's evaluation of the student.

The committee suggested we try to help the teachers to solve the problem. Actually, it was a program to help teachers help students in a very professional way. It also gave me a handle on the pulse of the school. This committee became a very vital part of what I did as a principal. It was a chance for me to show the teachers that I cared about them and that somebody was there to help them. Sometimes, we helped the teachers; sometimes, we could not, and the student was referred to the Special Education Child Study Team, but at least we tried.

The teachers in this school knew I was born again. I was trying to set an example of how a Christian teacher could share God's love by caring about the progress of the children in their classes. I met with this group until I retired, which was for about nine years. One of the other programs that came out of this committee was that they wanted to do a program to take one child who was having trouble and make him someone's friend so that they could help that child. This is above and beyond what was required of them. This kind of situation added to the atmosphere of the school. We all had a need to care not only for the children but also for the teachers and the parents. Parents were a big part of this picture. I continued to have meetings with the parents on a parenting program where parents could share what they did that was working with their child. It was very effective! I found that working on the attitudes of love in a caring environment made it a joy to come to school every day. I could tell the teachers enjoyed working in that atmosphere. One teacher I would like to mention here was Mary.

As I mentioned previously, Mary at one time was a supervisor in the district but now wanted to go back and teach. When she was a supervisor, I had a meeting with her, and when the meeting was over, I walked to my car, and the Lord spoke to me in my heart and told me to invite Mary to one of the Full Gospel meetings that I played at in Tommy's restaurant.

So I walked back, and I really did not want to ask her because she was my supervisor, but I did what I was told. When she got there, I greeted her and found a seat for her. She seemed to be happy. We played all our music in that group, By the Grace of God, and I could tell she was enjoying the music. At the end, Pastor Walt gave the sermon, and she took the altar call, and I was so happy. She thanked me for inviting her, and I saw a change in her attitude, and that was good. Mary and I have been close friends ever since. She went home to be with the Lord a couple of years ago. Before she died, she told me that her Black friend that she brought to one of the meetings was now a pastor of a church.

Saint Aloysius

We had one other part of the Holman School that was in the empty Catholic school. The board of education rented the school, and we had our kindergarten and first grades in that school. I would go over to that school once a day, and it was great for me to see the kids and the teachers, who were very loving and encouraging people. This was a great atmosphere for little children. It also was a great atmosphere for the principal, who would go in the church and meditate and get what he needed in a quiet place away from the hustle and bustle.

We all worked on the environment of this school, and it was a peaceful workplace. I was not apprehensive at all about coming to work in this school.

The district had a buyout to encourage people to retire, and I decided to take that retirement to save the district money. I really did not want to retire. I liked what I was doing, but I was also feeling the nudge inside again; however, I had no plan. I tried to back out, but the superintendent told me it was too late.

1. Psalm 45: When you fill your life with God's Word, it is a mighty weapon against the enemy. Psalm

45:2 (KJV), "Thou art fairer than the children of men: grace is poured into thy lips: therefore God hath blessed thee for ever."

Teachers who have a heart for children have grace poured out their lips. These teachers who were working on this committee had the blessing of God. They truly wanted to help teachers who wanted to help children. It was a blessing for me to be associated with a group of teachers who would accept coaching from another teacher to improve the progress of a student.

2. First Corinthians 13:4 (NIV), "Love is patient, love is kind. It does not envy, it does not boast, it is not proud."

I tried very hard not to judge what was going on in this committee and tried to show kindness to them all. This was definitely a mission of love, what these teachers accomplished, and there was no one who boasted about what they accomplished.

This was a lesson not only for the teachers but also for me. This climate was very safe for them to help each other. Only in a Christ-like climate could this happen. What came out was the highest complement of professionalism and teachers' respect and love for each other. With the Christ-like atmosphere, teachers respected the opinion of other teachers without the principal judging them.

While that was going on in the school, I had some meetings with parents about their children where I used the handbook I developed from the last school I was at. Parents loved talking about their children and listening to stories about how parents dealt with the problems they were dealing with.

This was the last school I remember working in and a memorable one. The atmosphere in the school was very caring and supportive to parents and the principal. I will never forget the flag somebody brought in so that I could let the buses go for the last time. I will never forget the faces looking out the bus window as their principal road off into the sunset.

CHAPTER SIX

By the Grace of God Singing Group

From the Flame of Love Prayer Meeting came our singing group called By the Grace of God. We sang at the prayer meetings, which led to people recommending this singing group to other churches and prayer meetings. The word got out about us, so we also sang in many of the churches in Toms River, New Jersey. We were asked to sing at a Christian dinner club once a month in a local restaurant as a warm-up group for a more popular singing group.

This group, By the Grace of God, was our way of supporting the local churches. It became inspiring to us as we shared our testimony from time to time. We gave our hearts to Jesus, and we were encouraged to support the local churches.

We did not know what would become of this ministry we had, but we were very inspired by the Holy Spirit to do whatever we could for the body of Christ. We gave up time away from our families to support this ministry. It was surely a joy to go to various churches as ambassadors of Jesus, and it changed my life.

One of the prayer meetings we supported was in Linden, New Jersey. That church was St. John Church. Sal's father was a member of that community. We went there with the love of Jesus and got back a lot more than we had brought.

Something that we learned was that we gave to these communities and received so many blessings.

Weddings

We served at two weddings, and I felt that the Holy Spirit was present at the wedding ceremony. The people who got married received a blessing along with the people who played the music. To me, weddings are special, and it was an honor for us to participate.

Jewish Community

When I was principal of the Johnson School, the music teacher Barry Rosenswage was also the music director at Beth Israel Synagogue in Lakewood, New Jersey. I asked Barry if his congregation would like to have some biblical music presented to them at a social.

The rabbi wanted to see the music, so we picked out all the music that was from the Old Testament.

The rabbi approved, and a meeting was set up. When we got to the synagogue, the people who worshiped there were a little apprehensive. So we were very friendly and loving to them with little response. You could tell they did not know what to expect. As the evening continued, the congregation started to loosen up, and they were getting very friendly. When we played "Halva Nigella," they were dancing on the floor.

They could not do enough for us! What a lesson learned for them and us. We gave them love, and we got it back from them.

Men's Full Gospel Outreach #2

One of the men in the Full Gospel asked us to sing at their meetings, which took place once a month in Tommy's restaurant. We agreed, and this was another wonderful outreach for the body of Christ. Men took other men to a meeting at a restaurant, and the person bringing a man paid for the dinner. Pastor Walt Healy was the minister and gave a teaching, at the end he gave an opportunity for an altar call.

Jay and Mike's Restaurant in Jackson, New Jersey

This was another outreach on a Friday night to go out to dinner and listen to gospel music. This was one more outreach in Ocean County.

Point Pleasant Christmas Outdoor Party

We played for a Christmas party for the town of Point Pleasant, New Jersey. We brought gospel music to a Christmas party for a town.

All in all, we played for about four years in the By the Grace of God Ministry. We were then asked to play for the Grace and Peace Church.

1. Philippians 4:13 (KJV), "I can do all things through Christ which strengtheneth me."

We were three people who had a heart for Jesus and wanted to do what we could for the body of Christ. We learned and played and gave our hearts and time to the one who needed us at that time.

Ocean County needed spirit-filled music, and we did it in the name of Jesus.

2. Men's Full Gospel. John 14:6 (NIV), "I am the way and the truth and the life. No one comes to the Father except through me."

The men at the Full Gospel were given the opportunity to accept Jesus as their savior and live for an eternity. Many men did and returned to the local churches to be fed.

CHAPTER SEVEN

The Church of Grace and Peace

While this was taking place, Walt Healy called Sal and Joan over to his house and told us he was starting a church. He wanted to know if we wanted to minister for that church. We were thrilled, but this meant that it would leave little time for us to do the ministry of By the Grace of God. We thought it over and said yes, and he told us we would be in the middle school in Toms River. Our mission was set; we were to get the music together and learn many new songs for worship at the new church.

The new church was called Grace and Peace. We had to move our equipment in and out of the church every Sunday and then break it down and take it back home. The church grew and grew until it was ready for us to get in a building. There were about twenty-five of us who signed papers that we put our house as collateral for a short period of time. The land that the church is on now was a farm, and we practiced our music at the farmhouse. The services were held in the middle school. It was an exciting time. When we built the church, we had many young people who wanted to be in the music ministry, which was good.

I dropped out to do Sunday school with my wife for about four years. Lisa and Steve Martin were on the staff. The church was built, and they did not have room for the children; now, there were about one hundred to 150 children. They rented buses to take the children to the middle school every week. I took the children on buses to the middle school. I was qualified and trained due to all those years as a principal, so it was an easy chore. I don't think a layperson without experience could do that. This was the Lord's timing to move out of the music ministry and then head of the Sunday school. Soon after my wife and I started doing Sunday school, my wife was diagnosed with breast cancer, so we dropped out of that ministry and had to take care of this problem.

This was a scary time for us, and now we had to hold on to the Lord real tight. We were fairly new born-again Christians, and we were kind of confused that this happened to us. We prayed that the Lord would heal my wife, and He did. In one year, she was cancer-free; we were very happy.

In 2005, cancer was back in the other breast. This was another operation, and it was successful again. Thank the Lord. By now, she had developed emphysema, and that was a tough one to beat. Long story short, with the help of the Lord, she beat cancer three times, but the emphysema was taking hold of her. I dropped out of all activities and took care of Irene until she went to the Lord in 2017. We often talked about her in heaven and me meeting her under the apple tree. We got a good chuckle out of that.

At one time, the principal of the academy, which was the school for the church, had a heart attack. At the time, I was on the board for the school. I knew right away that they would not have a principal for the school for the next couple of weeks. I told the board that I would do it since I had the credentials. This was a delightful assignment. It was a great school where children learned in an environment that I was trying to create in the public school. I really enjoyed being with the staff and teachers in that school. It was a joy!

1. Second Corinthians 13:11 (NIV), "Finally, brothers and sisters, rejoice. Strive for full restoration, encourage one another, be of one mind, live in peace, and the God of love and peace will be with you."

Pastor Walt was very encouraging to us and told us how pleased he was with our ministry. This, to us, was a big deal; we knew that this church would be successful. I never knew a man that knew the Scripture as he did. If anybody could encourage a group of believers to be of one mind, it would be Pastor Walt.

When Pastor Walt went home this year, Pastor Jim Wehrer had been senior pastor, so it was a very easy transition. When I was principal of the academy because the regular principal had a heart attack, I would go into the church to listen to Pastor Jim preach to the children in the academy, and I would say to myself, *What a good teacher of the Word he is; I know the church is in good hands.* Pastor James and Pastor Freda are to assist him, and all I could think of about this team is that they are an asset to the gospel of Jesus.

2. Acts 20:24 (KJV), "But none of these things move me, neither count I my life dear unto myself, so that I might finish my course with joy, and the ministry, which I have received of the Lord Jesus, to testify the gospel of the grace of God."

We knew that Pastor Walt had been given a gift to preach and teach the gospel of the Lord Jesus and to testify the gospel of the grace of God. It was a privilege to serve God under the teaching and instruction of Pastor Walt. We carried the equipment into the middle school every Sunday, set it up, and took it down for at least four years until the church was built. By the Grace of God singing group became a larger group of musicians and singers. I stayed until I knew it was time for me to help Irene (my wife) in the Sunday school.

3. Matthew 4:23 (KJV), "And Jesus went about all Galilee, teaching in their synagogues, and preaching the gospel of the kingdom, and healing all manner of sickness and all manner of disease among the people."

In her life, Irene was healed three times for cancer, twice in her breast and once on the back of her neck. The illness that lingered was emphysema. I had to think about why she was healed of cancer and not emphysema.

CHAPTER EIGHT

Retired

When I retired from public education, the Jackson board of education participated in a state program that allowed them to retire educators by adding five years to their retirement package. I decided I would take the package. It sounded very good. The only thing was I was not ready to retire. I was only fifty-seven years old, so I tried to drop out of the retirement program but was told I could not once I told them I would take it.

I will never forget the last day of school for me. It was bittersweet. I liked the sound of retirement, but I was in love with what I was doing in education. I knew my position was a ministry, and I looked at it as that. Again, I felt the nudge inside when I took the package. That last day, the teachers gave me a flag that they use in car races, and I stood on the bus ramp waving this big flag at each bus as they passed, and the kids were all waving to me as the buses pulled out. I was almost sad to be leaving something I loved to do. I will never forget that day.

Soon after that scene, I rushed home, and my wife was waiting for me to go out to dinner to celebrate. She knew I would feel sad after so many years working with children and teachers.

I would say about a week after I retired, I called a friend of mine who had retired as a superintendent of a school and had taken a position as department chair in education at Monmouth University. I asked him if he needed any professors to teach. He hired me. I had done many workshops for the district where he worked, so he was delighted to hire me.

Monmouth University

On my first day at Monmouth, I had to pinch myself. I could not believe I was teaching at a college. I was well prepared with all the experience. I had twenty-eight years as a principal and had learned many different programs that Jackson Township made us all do. Now I could share this good information plus experience with young people who were going to be future teachers.

This was not only a good experience for the students, it was also a great experience for me to share my experience. The Lord put me in a good position to help young people who would help the children they taught.

One of the interesting stories when I taught there was when I took my grandchildren to a football game. I had one of the players in my class, and he gave me tickets. My grandchildren were about five and seven years old, and they loved football. I could remember sitting in the end zone, and Monmouth was about to score, and I could not get their attention. They were playing their own game in the end zone while their grandfather cheered on Monmouth University.

I had an online doctorate degree, and at this time, they would not hear about that kind of program. I enrolled in Widener University in a doctoral program and traveled to Philadelphia once a week for my coursework. I finished all my coursework and passed the comprehensive test and only needed to complete my thesis for the program. My son needed me in a business he was in, and finances were a concern. The doctoral at my age at the time did not seem to be a good idea.

The business did not do well, as there was a mortgage crash, and all businesses were in trouble.

Concurrently my wife was getting worse, and I was giving more time to her.

1. Interesting point of view. When it's time to move on, the Lord may have something else in mind for you. In this case, I was sorry to leave the school, but a whole new world opened up for me, teaching at Monmouth University. We have to remember that the Lord is in control, and sometimes we have to let go and let Him do what

He does best and not try to control everything in life. It was a dream of mine to teach what I had learned in thirty-three years in education to younger teachers in Monmouth who, when they heard I was a principal, were in awe of my experience. The Lord blessed me because this was one of the highlights of my career. Little did I know the point is that many times, what looks like a closed door is a wide-open life. Praise the Lord!

2. One important point I would like to make. I knew what my purpose in life was, although, in my younger days, I would not think it. My purpose was to work with children and teach in public schools. I was very successful at that, and I knew that. There were times when I had an opportunity to get in other businesses. I did that on a limited basis because I was not successful at some of the things I did. One of the things I did was to get in business with my son to help him, and it was a mortgage business. That was the crash of 2008, and that was not successful. The point I am making is that when you know what you are good at or when you know the Lord gave you the talent to do something, it is a good idea to follow through with that talent. I did that a couple of times, and it did work out.

Family

After the two girls were born, we decided to look for a house in south Jersey. We were looking for an area that had a good school system and was a nice community. We settled for a planned community in Howell Township, New Jersey, which was next to Lakewood, New Jersey. I accepted a Job in Jackson Township that was about twenty minutes from my home. We had a struggle at the beginning when we first moved. We used part of the down payment from the money we received for working in the summer. So I was faced with a dilemma that was we did not have enough money to live or for food. We were blessed with a good job, and if I had to work, it would be only for the summer. The only job at such a late date for me was to load trucks in Jersey City. I got on a bus from Howell, and my friend Ralph also was with me. He moved to Freehold, and we both went up to Jersey City to work. The most difficult job I ever had. We both got through the summer. Ralph took a job in Matawan. We were both blessed to have a new home and a new job to start the school year. I will be ever so grateful that the Lord gave me the nudge to move on for my family and me. My family attended a church in Howell by the name of St. Veronica. We were not involved in that church, but I made sure we got to church every Sunday.

I mentioned in another chapter some of the episodes that happened, but things started to change in my family when my mother had cancer and I did not have anybody to take care of her. My wife, Irene, said she would take the girls up to Jersey City and take care of my mother. I would live at home and come up every other day. My mother passed in 1969, and it feels like yesterday. It was the same time as the moon landing. My mother witnessed that, and soon after that, about a week, she passed. The following year, my son John was born; now, I had two girls and one boy.

As I stated before, Irene and I went to a marriage encounter, and both of us were touched by His love. One of the themes for the weekend was Ephesians 5.

Ephesians 5 (GNT):

> Submit yourselves to one another because of your reverence for Christ. Wives submit yourselves to your husband as to the Lord.
> For a husband has authority over his wife just as Christ has authority over the church and Christ himself the Savior of the church, his body. And so wives must submit themselves completely their husbands just as the church submits itself to Christ.
> Husbands love your wives just as Christ loved the church and gave his life for it. He did this

> to dedicate the church to God by his word
> after making it clean by washing it in water,
> in order to present the church to himself in all
> its beauty—pure and faultless without spot or
> wrinkle or any other imperfection. Men ought
> to love their wives just as they love their own
> bodies a man who loves his wife loves himself.
> No one hates his own body, but feeds and take
> care of it. And that is what Christ does for the
> church because we are part of his body.

In this seminar, we were taught to submit to one another. Sometimes the ladies at this seminar had a problem with submitting to their husband, but it's a mutual submission. What my wife and I experienced in this kind of relationship was a different kind of love. It was a God kind of love. It was a beautiful relationship. When you think of it, we both had given our hearts to the Lord, and we were both in love with each other. How can you top that! We had this unconditional love; this was the best experience we had as a married couple. It was a love we had for God and a love He had for us. How could you not want this for a relationship?

Agape (Wikipedia): agape (Ancient Greek ἀγάπη, agapē) is a Greco-Christian term referring to unconditional love, "the highest form of love, charity"

and "the love of God for man and of man for God."
Agape.

This love was unconditional; we both took care of each other, and I knew she had the same love I had for her.

I could feel the love of God in my wife. We joined the prayer community, and I could remember one elderly man who would call my wife the Holy Spirit. She had tears in her eyes at all the services. She was truly touched by the Holy Spirit, and I felt from her the love of God. How can a couple lose when a wife and the husband have Jesus in their lives and both are looking out for the other person? When we were having a hard financial time, Irene would always make sure the children were taken care of, and then me, and she was last. I know that this book is a testimony of my life and how Jesus influenced my life; if there is one thing you must get is the agape love that I explained in this chapter. The most important incident that ever happened to me was when I accepted Jesus in my heart. The next best thing was when my wife accepted Jesus, and we developed an extended love affair. We had agape love, which is the God kind of love.

My children would think it was the same Mom and Dad, but I knew it was different. If only you could wrap it up and take that kind of situation out when you wanted it, but that's not how life is. Sometimes we are on the mountain, and sometimes we are in the valley. It affects us, but God never changes. Those are the lessons we have to learn in life to hold on to Him even when we are in the valley. As I get older, I do rely on Him more and more each day.

Children, Patty and Carol

We did what most people did with our kind of prayer before they went to bed. I had a little thing I did with my girls, and that was I told them stories about Patty and Carol; it was really them, and they knew it. They also knew I was making them up, but I was using real-life situations to teach them behavior. I would do this once a week, and we called it "treat night." I would lie down and put them to sleep, telling them stories. These stories sometimes times were funny, and we had a good time, but sometimes, they were more serious and about how to treat their girlfriends.

Sometimes, it was how they treated their mother or me.

George Amabile, Dad

Goetz Middle School

H.C. Johnson Elementary School

Holeman Staff

Jackson Memorial High School

John and Ralph, 18 years old, Wildwood, New Jersey

JT Kounelias, Kortney

Karen Amabile Russo, Jake Russo

John and Irene Amabile, Honeymoon, Lakewood, NJ

Justin and Victoria Kounelias

Holeman Elementary

Mom and Dad Amabile

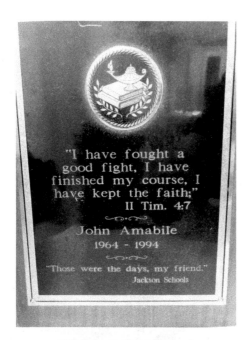

Gift from Jackson Schools

Ralph and John, Graduating Seton Hall University

St. Michael's Church, Jersey City

*Coach Amabile and Jackson Memorial High School
Football Team*

The Four Ivy's Northwest Missouri State University

John, Joan, Sal
By the Grace of God music ministers

Mom and Dad walking with John on Newark Avenue,
Jersey City

Son, John Amabile; Wife, Jennifer; Daughters, Ava and Faith

John Amabile and Ralph Guadagno

CHAPTER NINE

Family

Family Meeting

The things I learned in education and put in at least three schools was a class meeting. I would require the teacher to sit down with their class and meet with the children to find out many things like who needed help or maybe just to pat somebody on the back or just talk. Rules were easy; you could bring up any subject as long as it was helping in some way. The students would raise their hands if they wanted to speak, and they could not use any Killer statements. Killer statements were any kind of put-down. Once the teachers got a handle on these meetings, they really liked them.

Getting back to my family—what does this have to do with them? I required my children to be home for supper every night. We had to eat together. At the dinner table, they would talk about their day, and if anything went wrong, it was usually brought out. My kids thought I was acting like a principal, and sometimes they were not too cooperative.

Winding River

We moved to Toms River in the '70s, and what a nice location. The Toms River Stream was behind my house, and that area was a city park called Winding River Park. When I look back at this location and the house, this was from God. I was into running, so I ran down the park almost every day. Then sometimes, I would walk with my two girls down the park. That activity carried over. They still walk every day when they can. You could walk at least five miles in that park. It was beautiful; it is still beautiful. Not only was there good walking, but there was a stream, a big stream; it was the beginning of the Toms River. We canoed down the river, did water rafting; it was just a fun place to live.

Children Bible Study

When my wife and I got involved with the prayer community, we felt a need to have a Bible study in my house. We contacted the young pastor at the Assembly of God Church, and he did a Bible study at my house. We had a beautiful living room with a fireplace that was unique. It was made of stone. A football coach friend had a boy on his team whose father was a mason. He gave me his name. He was not only a mason; he was also an artist. Imagine a big stone fireplace, driftwood mantle, cooper arches, just beautiful. We had about five boys and girls come over to my house every week, and it was joyous. It was a great setting for the work of God to be discussed with young people. Irene and I felt very good about this meeting; it was excellent for our children.

Vacation Time for our Children

It was about this time I wanted to take the children on vacation, and we decided to go to Disney in Florida. I could not go to the hotels because it was too expensive, so I decided to get a pop-up camper and camp in Disney World.

I think this was the first time it was open. We had a great time, not only at Disney but also camping out. The kids thought this was great! On our way back from Disney, we stopped at our friends' house. They were just moving in. Their house was in Florida, and we had a great visit with them. Their names are Larry and Carol D'Zio. Larry was the baseball coach at the high school, and Carol was the cheerleading coach and English teacher. Larry was a history teacher.

One other trip was when we went down to see my sister in North Carolina and stopped at Cape Hatteras. This was so interesting for them. We went to the Wright Brothers Museum and camped on the beach in the Cape. It was interesting. There was one time that reminded

BY THE GRACE OF GOD

me of when Jesus told Thomas to throw the net over the side for fish, and he said he had done that already; when he did, he got hundreds of fish. I was showing my son how to fish, but I had never done that before. The lure had about twenty hooks on it. Every time we threw the lure in the water, we had about twenty fish on the end. I had never seen anything like that. I was fishing in a school of fish. About that time, a storm was coming, and we had a bucket of fish. We picked up our equipment and went back to the campsite, and it really started to pour. We left the bucket on the table and got in the station wagon. When it stopped raining, we looked out back, and the seagulls were eating our fish. I had a crying little boy I had to deal with. I tried to give him tuna in a can, but he did not buy that. I had to buy him something he liked to make him happy.

The next year I bought a self-contained camper. To us, this was a wonderful mobile home. Now, where to? We decided to go across the country to California.

California

It was such a great idea to expose our kids to places other than New Jersey. We went through the badlands and Mount Rushmore, which was a wonderful experience. Then, we went to Yellowstone, which you can't put into words. Yellowstone is a good example of God's work on earth; it was breathtaking. There were high mountains, beautiful sunsets, animals all over, and of course, Old Faithful and springs that never stopped giving. Just a great experience to show our children the majesty of God. When we got to Kansas, I told the kids we were going to see some of my college friends, so we did not go all the way to California. I think they were happy, as they were getting a little tired of the road trip and camping with their parents.

We went east to Topeka, Kansas, where I had a dear friend, Jerry Overton, who had just bought the house from the president of the college in Topeka, and it was beautiful. There was no furniture in the mansion, but it had carpeting throughout. There were about eight adults with all their children. These were all my friends from college. What an exciting time. Jim Taylor was there. He was the guy that took me up to my college and introduced me to the coach in Maryville. We slept on the floor; the kids thought that it was great to see all these people sleeping on the floor. All in all, it was a great time.

From there, we went up to my college, where Irene and I lived for a year and a half. The kids were not too thrilled with that, but we were. From there, we headed home, which was about 1200 miles. We stopped a couple of times, and the children went swimming, and we had a good meal.

After the camping episodes, the girls were getting older and wanted to go to the ocean with their friends, so the camping was out.

Two Bible teachings we instilled in our children. One is "You reap what you sow." They knew this principle very well. If you want good grades, you must put in the time; if you want to be a good athlete, you must practice.

The other principle is that "God is love." When we came back from our marriage encounter seminar, we made sure they knew 1 Corinthians 13, the definition that Paul gave to love.

First Corinthians 13:1–8 (AMP):

The Excellence of Love
If I speak with the tongues of men and of angels but have no love (for others growing out of God's love for me), then I have become only a noisy gong or a clanging cymbal (just an annoying distraction). And if I have the gift of prophecy (and speak a new message from God to the people) and understand all mysteries and (possess) all knowledge; and if I have all (sufficient) faith so that I can remove mountains, but do not have love (reaching out to others), I am nothing. If I give all my possessions to feed the poor, and if I surrender my body to be burned but do not have love, it does me no good at all.

Love endures with patience and serenity...;
love does not brag and is not pound or
arrogant. It is not rude; it is not self-seeking,
it is not provoked (nor overly sensitive and
easily angered); it does not consider a wrong
endured. It does not rejoice at injustice but
rejoices with the truth (when right and truth
prevail). Love bears all things (regardless
of what comes), believes all things (looking
for the best in each one), hopes all things
(remaining steadfast during difficult times),
endures all things (without weakening).
Love never fails (it never fades nor ends). But
as for prophecies, they will pass away, and as
for tongues, they will cease as for the gift of
special knowledge, it will pass away.

Paul's definition of love is looked upon as a literary
masterpiece. Irene and I tried in our way to show the
love of Jesus in all the things we did with our children.
Irene became the disciplining parent; she was home
with them all the time. But we tried to discipline them
in the best way we knew how, and that was with love.
Sometimes they did not see it that way, but sometimes
as parents, you have to take a stance on certain issues.

Our Son

John was very close to me. I took him everywhere with me; he knew all my friends and was such a loving little boy. When he was of age, he wanted to play little league, so I volunteered to be a coach. Dad was a football coach when I worked at the high school, so I thought this would be a snap. I tried to show John if he wanted to pitch, he had to practice at least half an hour a day to be good at it. We practiced with the team once a week and played a game once a week. I worked with John for at least half a day catching with him in the backyard, which he loved. A funny thing about catching in the backyard was when I missed one of my pitches, it hit the back wall and broke one of the tiles on the siding. You could have imagined what the wall looked like when we moved. I had to replace half of the back siding. He became a good little pitcher who struck out twelve batters in one game.

Our next challenge was when he wanted to play Pop Warner Football. So again, I worked with him every day, and at the age of fourteen, he could throw a football at least forty-five yards. He was a very good quarterback. Then, he got turned off to football and all sports and became involved with a spiritual group at his school. He went to St. Joseph Catholic School in Toms River. He helped out by running a seminar called "Search for Children" and also learned how to play guitar and played as a music minister for this group. He still plays as a music minister for the Episcopal Church in Red Bank.

John is now married to Jennifer, and they have two beautiful girls inside and out.

Life Guard

John and Jennifer are part of a foundation in Monmouth County called Life Guard. This is a group of people who raise money to help the needy. They have yard sales and have concerts to raise money to help people who need to pay rent or maybe need money for an operation, whatever they need. Sometimes they might buy a car for somebody who does not have a way to get to work. They are a great group of people who have a heart for God and want to make a difference. I can't say enough about these people who give up their time to raise money to help other people. They not only give up their time but also the children of all these people are involved. What a learning experience of helping others. This scripture says it all:

Matthew 5:8 (ESV), "Blessed are the pure at heart, for they shall see God."

These are families helping other families. What a wonderful concept. What if our world was set up as is with the heart of God?

Our Girls

Irene and Mike Fisher moved to South Carolina because of climate change for medical reasons. Mike has had two operations on his back, and the weather is better in that area.

Karen is a special education teacher in Jersey City and lives in Bayonne, New Jersey. Both girls graduated from Georgian Court University with a bachelor's degree and a master's degree from Concordia College.

Irene, My Wife

In 1982, Irene had an occurrence of breast cancer, and we were in shock. We went to our regular doctor, and he told us we needed a specialist. I wanted the best for her, and at that time, Sloan Kettering was the best. So we called and made an appointment to see a doctor, and the doctor they gave us was the head of the department at Sloan Kettering. I think the Lord had something to do with that. We met with the doctor, and he told us that he would not know if the breast had to be removed until he looked at it in the operating room. So we made the appointment and planned to go to New York for the operation. I slept at home, so I traveled up the day of the operation. I can remember waiting in the lobby and getting anxious, so I went outside and walked the streets of New York like the world was coming to an end. I was in a daze. I did not want to lose Irene; I loved her. I felt like I was in a movie and that this was not happening. At that time, not too many people survived cancer.

Finally, I went back to the hospital and met with the doctor. He told me that the cancer did not spread, but he had to take the breast. I knew she would not be happy, but she was going to live. She was not happy about losing a breast. I was very happy about her living. Thank You, Jesus.

Irene had a hard time dealing with the fact that she did not have a breast. That was the beginning of the trend to take the breast so women would survive.

Moving about twenty-five years ahead (2005), we had another scare; there was another breast problem. This time we went to a local doctor, and it was a lot easier. We did not have to travel, and we knew what to expect. It was stage four, and this gave us a scare. Our prayer team at the church prayed for her, and the doctor told me that he did not think any of the cancer was left, but she needed radiation treatments.

Two years later, it was cancer on the back of the neck. She had cancer three times, and three times she was healed. The doctor removed the cancer, and she was all right.

The biggest problem was the emphysema she had while she had all that cancer. This was the result of smoking when she was younger. When the doctor told us that she had emphysema and that there was no cure, it was a shock after beating cancer so many times. She made me promise that I would not put her in a nursing home and I would take care of her at home. I never wanted to put her in the nursing home anyway. I felt I made a commitment fifty-nine years ago that I would take care of her till death do us part. In June of 2017, Irene passed to be with the Lord, and she was at home; the children and I took care of her.

Celebrating the Life of Irene

We wanted her parting to be a celebration of the life of Irene Amabile. The pastor gave a very heartwarming talk, and he also used the time to tell the people there about the hereafter; Dee Graziano gave a little talk about Irene as a girlfriend, and Jerry Tiegh talked about Irene as a neighbor.

My grandchildren read scripture. Psalm 23 was a favorite of Irene, and 1 Corinthians 13 was another one that another grandchild read.

The repose after the church service was at the restaurant at the development, and there were about eighty people there. It was a celebration of Irene's life. Her family was there, and it was comforting to see all our friends and family giving my kids and me the love they gave. The next chapter in my life was to settle down and decide what to do with my life. We had discussions about when we died and what we would do. We decided that if she died after this illness, she wanted me to go on with my life.

A New Direction for My Life

Now, I was living in a house that was 2600 square feet, and that was too big and too expensive for me.

I knew I needed to sell my home and move into a smaller house. My children were married and lived where they worked. Karen was working as a special education teacher in Jersey City and living in Bayonne. My son was living in Fair Haven, and Irene in South Carolina. I was alone, and it would be a good move for me to move into something smaller. My brother George is a realtor, so I called him in and told him that I wanted to sell my home, and he listed my house. I did not get a buyer for a whole year, and I knew something was wrong. One day, I sat in my bedroom and talked to the Lord. I asked Him to help me and what I should do. I did not hear words but what came into my mind was "add another room." My bedroom was oversized because I made an office out of it. I made a beautiful room out of the space I had. I called a friend of the family, and he came up with a plan, and I said okay, and it came out beautiful.

We made the room to the building code, and it looked great. Rather than use my brother, I used a local realtor, and when we put it up for sale, we had three bids for the house for the price I wanted. This was the favor of God. We went from nobody wanting the house to getting three bids.

Now I had to find a home that was suitable for me. I looked in a community in the Toms River area and came upon a home that had great possibilities. I fixed an old house up to look new, and I am enjoying living in a smaller home. It's very comfortable.

This did not solve my spiritual desire. I knew there was something for me to do. I was happy but did not have the joy of the Lord in my life. I struggled with living alone. I was married for fifty-nine years with one lady, and now I was alone. I did more praying; I listened to more music, and I asked the Lord what He wanted me to do with my life. I thought I might leave a legacy for my children, so I started, and it came easy. Then, He wrote on my heart that "If I did all these things for you, why don't you share this with other people other than yourself?" So I did. I brought it to the life group at our church, and it seemed to go pretty well. I put it down and started to forget what I had set out to do, and the Lord said to me to put it in the form of a book. I told him I really was tired of the academic part of writing. I had done this all my life, and it did not come easy. He asked me the question, "Are you happy with what I did for you? Then why won't you share it with other people?" Then, He said, "You are not too old."

I'm writing this book so that maybe someone will be touched, and maybe they will pick up their talent and glorify the Lord. I hear so many preachers say there are many people who died still having all the talent the Lord gave them, and they never developed. When I was a principal, I encouraged teachers to develop and to come up with new ideas. I also encouraged them to encourage young people. We all have an obligation to develop what talent we have in the name of the Lord. My prayer is that you look back at your life to see God's favor and recognize it in your past so that you can see it in the here and now. The more I looked, the more I found, and now, when it comes, I see it and recognize when God is working in your life for you. God is working in your life by faith. Romans 10:17 (KJV), "So then faith cometh by hearing, and hearing by the word of God."

Whenever I am looking for answers to questions, I look to the Word of God. If you are searching for your talent, look to the Word. If you know what your talent is, look to the Word to see what you can do to reach your goal.

Legacy

It is a good idea to write a legacy. With the nucleus of the family spread so far apart, today, it is hard to get together. So the legacy would be a way to communicate what you want your kids to know about your beliefs.

You can write a book like I am doing, or you can write a paper. Some people put it on video. The point is to get your message across.

My son and I facetime at least once a day, sometimes in the late evening, just to chat.

CHAPTER TEN

Final

The dictionary definition of favor of God is often looked upon as the grace of God. God shows favoritism to those who have faith and give honor to Him.

Isaiah 66:2 (GNT), "I myself created the whole universe! I am pleased with those who are humbled and repentant, who fear me and obey me."

Isaiah 66:2 (ESV), "But this is the one to whom I will look: he who is humble and contrite in spirit and trembles at my word."

To have favor, you must have faith that there is a God. Be humble and contrite in spirit and fear not keeping His word. In 2 Chronicles 16:9 (AMPC), He says, "For the eyes of the Lord run to and fro through the whole earth to give favor to those whose heart are blameless..."

To be perfect in Him means to seek Him more than anything in the world, and He will give you favor.

When I researched favor, I found out that many scholars say that favor is closely related to grace. Some say that the term is interchangeable. Grace came with the coming of Jesus and the crucifixion. We now live in a time of grace.

John 1:17 (ESV), "For the law was given through Moses and Grace and Truth came through Jesus Christ."

We are now born in a time of Grace. God's message is a message of grace. God is willing to forgive us for the sins that we were born with.

Psalm 51:5 (GNT), "I have been evil from the day I was born; from the time I was conceived I have been sinful."

This scripture shows that we were born with sin and have a sinful nature.

When Jesus died and was buried and rose again on the third day, He brought with Him grace. We are in a period of grace because of the crucifixion of Jesus. This was the sacrifice of the Lamb. Before this, we lived by the law.

Favor and Grace

I am going to show some of the favor God put on my life, but before I do, I would like to quote scripture that will help me.

Psalm 30:4 (ESV):

> Sing praises to the Lord O you his saints
> And give thanks to his Holy Name
> for his anger is but for a moment
> And his favor is for a lifetime.

It goes on to say that joy comes in the morning. It is important to note that God's favor is for a lifetime. We all have favor; we need to humble ourselves and receive it.

Second Chronicles 33:12 (NIV), "In his distress he [Manseiah] sought the favor of the Lord his God and humbled himself greatly before the God of his ancestors."

The point here is that for a person to receive favor, they humble themselves before God. Another point is that our God will give you favor for a lifetime.

Proverbs 3:3–4 (ESV):

> Let not steadfast love and faithfulness forsake you
> Bind them around your neck
> Write them on the tablet of your heart
> So you will find favor and good success
> In the sight of God and man.

The Lord is saying here to bind love and faithfulness around your neck, and you will find favor and good success. That seems like a food formula to practice love (with God); be faithful, and you will find favor and success. In my life, I have practiced love and found much success. I even used it in my job and tried to create an atmosphere of love and caring for children and parents.

Psalm 90:17 (ESV):

"Let the favor of the Lord our God be upon us,

"And establish the work of our hands upon us;

"Yes, establish the work of our hands."

I believe what the Lord is saying is that when we humble ourselves and ask for God's favor, the work that we do will be inspired by God. I marvel at some of the young Christian singers; their voices are unbelievable. God's favor in these people comes shining through. Sometimes, I get touched by the Holy Spirit, and it brings tears to my eyes. Praise the Lord for these young people who are aware of the favor of God and can use their talent for the ministry of the Lord. I can think of two young men in the Brooklyn Tabernacle Choir that touch my heart every time I hear them sing. When you get this kind of favor, it's your obligation to share God's grace with other people. These young people singing with all their hearts are as good as a good sermon.

Galatians 1:10 (RSV), "Am I now seeing the favor of men, or of God? Or am I trying to please men? If I were still pleasing men, I should not be a servant of Christ."

This is a very interesting reversal of favor. Paul is telling us not to be a people pleaser and look for the favor of man. To serve Christ, you must be faithful to His calling and look for favor from God. It is very easy to please people, especially close friends.

Examples of Favor in My Life

My family stepped up when my family (Mother, John, George, and Anita, young baby sister) needed money to live on. If something like that happened years ago, you were not covered by the company. That would be a different story today.

Our God is our Father, as stated in the Bible. The first prayer that Jesus taught us begins with "our Father who art in heaven."

In John, it is said, "For on him God the Father has placed a seal of approval" (John 6:27, NIV).

First Corinthians 8:6 (NIV), "Yet for us there is but one God, the Father, from whom all things came and for whom we live; and there is but one Lord, Jesus Christ, through whom all things came and through whom we live."

People Used by God to Show Favor

In all of these scriptures, the author refers to God as God the Father. It is my belief that God has the role of Father of us all. If you don't have a father, God becomes your Father. The only problem is you need a way to recognize this favor of God. When my father died and my uncle took me to the church to meet the priest, I believe in my young way that I felt his love. I dedicated my life at this point to service to the church. I was an altar boy, played an instrument in the band, helped with all funerals in the church. Something happened in my heart. Looking back at this, I believe this was the favor of God. My aunt and uncles stepped in right away to help with finances for food. I thank God for these people; they were a part of the plan of God. We pray, "our Father who art in heaven."

Uncle Mike

Uncle Mike offered to use his GI Bill to buy a house together with my mother. He put up the down payment; the rent would help pay for the mortgage. It was a three-family home, so it carried itself. The agreement was that my mother would pay him back when she could.

This was done out of the goodness of his heart, and he had a big heart. This is the same man that played baseball with me every day after he finished his mail route because I did not have a father. He helped make life easier for us by owning a home. Then to come up with the down payment, this man had much love in his heart. God blessed him with a nice family and a good wife who loved him to the end.

Uncle Nick

He also helped out; he worked on construction and made sure I had a job with him every summer I was off from school. I always made good money, and I helped my mother when I worked. He was in the Second World

War, and when he was stationed in the west, I believe it was Texas, he sent me a nice letter and about five coins and told me he got it from a cowboy. I was big on cowboys.

Uncle Joe

He was like a father to me; he was the one that took me to the church and introduced me to the priest. He lived with us for a while before he moved to Pennsylvania. He was a Marine and very strict. That didn't go over while he stayed in our house; we knew he meant well. Just very militaristic. One thing I can tell you about Uncle Joe is he was a big Yankees fan. He took me to a couple of games when I was about five years old, and I still remember. In that game, Joe DiMaggio hit a home run. What a thrill! My uncle's name was Joe Di Geronimo. Do you see the connection? Uncle Joe was an airplane mechanic in an island near Japan, and he would fix and give warplanes fuel in the Second World War.

Aunt Angie

Aunt Angie was like a sister to me growing up. She taught me all the dances of the '40s and was a lot of fun to be around. She also lived with us for a little while. She worked down the Harborside in Jersey City. This is the part of the city that I talked about before that looked like New York spilled over into New Jersey. She was a very good-looking lady. She married another Uncle Joe and had three children. A very important person in my life.

My Mother

My mother was a blessing to my brother and sister and to me. She made sure we had all we needed and tried to have a normal family. At times I thought that we were alone as children in the evening, but I am sure she would have liked to be with us. She sacrificed so much for her children; we became very close. She was very supportive of me when I wanted to go to college, the first in the family. She received much criticism because of the support she gave me in going away to college and getting married and finishing up my degree. She was tickled pink when I became a teacher in Jersey City and was happy to see me as a principal. She was a very special person in my life; she had the love of God in her life. You could feel it.

New Home

The Lord blessed us with a new home that was a three-family home, which made it easier for us. The two-family part of the house paid the mortgage payment, and my mother lived rent-free. That was the favor of God blessing our family. Now, we had to make enough money for food and gas and electricity. My mother worked for the local church as a cleaning lady for a few years until she got a job at RCA on an assembly line making radio tubes. This was a blessing, but we did not have family life during the week, as her job was from 4 p.m. to 12 a.m., which meant we would not see her for supper. All was good financially, rent-wise, and we had enough money for food. Thanks be to God!

New School

When we moved into the new house, we had to change schools. We now had to go to School Number 17. I can't tell you how nice these people were. My father's death was on the front page of the Jersey Journal, which was the local paper, and I had an idea that this new school showed God's love to us when we went there.

Mr. Kaplan made me captain of the crossing guards. At that time, they had students acting as crossing guards, and I was captain after my friend Ralph. I remember Mrs. Bain, who a very lovely person was and took time with me. Mrs. Field was a tough teacher, and everybody was afraid of her, but she was so nice to me.

Ralph Guadagno

Ralph was more like a brother to me. He made sure I was included in everything, and we had plans when I got to high school that we would be on the same team. Upon graduation, Ralph went into service and became an MP. I did not go into service and stayed home with my mother for that period of time until a year later, George Tardif gave me a call.

Ralph and I graduated at the same time and got jobs in Jersey City as teachers. We also coached football at Lincoln High, the school we both graduated from. My cousin was the head coach, and Ralph and I were his assistants. We both left Jersey City, and I went to Jackson and became a principal, and Ralph went to Matawan, New Jersey, and he was the principal in the high school. We both went to Seton Hall for our master's degrees. When we retired, we both went to Monmouth University to teach. Ralph coached young teachers in the field, and I was a professor there for about three years.

Our lives shadowed each other from elementary school to working at Monmouth University. Ralph was the big brother I never had. Not having a father, we talked about the future and counseled each other. God placed him in my life at the right time when I needed somebody I could talk to and trust. He always looked out for my best interest. Ralph died about two months after my wife Irene in 2017. I miss my best friend. Looking back at this relationship, I think this was a good sample of God's favor.

Joe Louro

Joe was another high school friend of mine who played on the football team that Ralph and I played on. In 1956, we both had graduated, and Joe was working for a mill company and knew how to install windows and doors. Joe helped me repair my mother's house, and I will be ever grateful. In recent years, we talked at least twice a month. He was president of the Builder Association in Monmouth County and was a part-owner of a very large construction company. He built a very large church in Freehold and did not charge the church for his service. The priest at the mass said, "We asked Joe to build a church, and he built a cathedral." Joe died one week after I last talked to him on October 29, and I remember him saying to me, "You are my second best friend; Ralph is my best friend." Joe had a great sense of humor.

Miss Winifred Sullivan

Miss Sullivan was another blessing in my life. My only regret is that I never told her that. She took a sincere interest in me in my senior year and really inspired me to do more with my life. She encouraged me to write something for the school yearbook, and I told her I didn't think I could and I did not want to disappoint her. She encouraged me, and I wrote a poem about how man is amazing and how creative we could be, but then we could make a bomb to blow up the entire world. Miss Sullivan loved the poem, and it was put in the yearbook, and I was so proud of that. This was one of the encouraging moments for me to decide to go to college. Now, I am sitting at a computer typing a book to be published by TBN. Two lessons: First, God's favor in terms of the interest Miss Sullivan had in me. God used Miss Sullivan to show me that I could do it; I didn't have to be afraid of writing. Secondly, the power teachers have encouraging young people. I will never get to tell her, but I used some of the Spirit in the schools I was principal. My daughter Karen is a teacher in Jersey City, and I told her to get the Word to her niece, who taught with her. What a role Miss Sullivan played in my life.

God uses people to bless us, and Miss Sullivan was a blessing giving me God's favor.

Uncle Veto

God placed many people in my life to keep me on track. Uncle Veto had an oil delivery business in that same downtown section of Jersey City. At a young age, he taught me not only how to drive this big oil truck but also how to deliver oil and deal with customers. I did that for about five years on Saturdays, from 8 a.m. in the morning till about 3 p.m. in the afternoon. I was a good help to him; he taught me how the real world is. Dealing with people, the weather; if it snowed and rained, people needed their oil for heat, so there was no time off. People relied on you for heat. He corrected me in the things I did wrong, and he told me in no uncertain term not to do it again. Good worldly education, but he also cared about me, and that was the good thing about the relationship. I later took over his business when he had a heart attack. This is the job in my youth that built a lot of my character. He was a good influence on my life, another example of God's favor.

Construction

I had many jobs in construction in the summertime; my two uncles were in construction, and I always had work. They were helping me, and they were also helping my mother because I gave her money from my paycheck.

Doremus Ave

This was my first job; it was a job to clean up a fire that burned up the oil tank on Doremus Ave in Newark. I'll never forget this job. It was around Christmas time on my Christmas vacation.

New Jersey Parkway

I worked on the parkway for many years in the summertime. This was a blessing.

Bayonne Extension Turnpike Bridge

This was probably the best job, yet it was a seven-days-a-week job to keep the cofferdam dry for the men to work in the morning.

Irene

I could mention so many more instances of favor, but the most important one was the one when I met my wife. I got on the elevator at a dance, and she introduced herself to me, and we were married for fifty-nine years. This was another sample of God's favor in my life. She was the best!

Walt Healy and Maureen

Their sacrifice to start a church was not easy. I had a good foundation in the Word, and I continued from day one in the Church of Grace.

Thank you to the new team of pastors at the Church of Grace and Peace. They continue the work of Walt and Maureen Healy. They have been a blessing to me in my growth.

All these people had a place in my life, and God's favor shined through them. Thank God for them. I am who I am from the encouragement of the Lord and certainly all the people I have mentioned in this book who encouraged me to keep moving.

Scriptures that Influenced My Life in the Last Forty-Six Years

When I got saved, there were scriptures that influenced me. I thought it only proper to mention some of the scripture I read and outlined. These were all underlined in my first Bibles.

Personal Doctrine

It is my contention that all the scripture I read played a big part in developing my personal doctrine. I went through the first Bible to the last Bible and listed what scriptures I outlined in each one. I could not do all of them, but you'll get the idea when you see the scripture. This is a very important part of this book. What you put in your heart, you will be. If you put the scriptures that made a difference in your life, this becomes your personal doctrine. As you read, underline what's important and go back from time to time to read them and make them a part of your life in whatever you do.

This was one of the first scriptures I outlined in my first Bible. "Follow me" had an effect on my life. At that time, I really did not understand what this meant, but I do now.

Matthew 4:18 (AMP):

> As Jesus was walking by the Sea of Galilee, He noticed two brothers, Simon, who was called Peter, and Andrew his brother, casting a net into the sea for they were fishermen. And He said to them, "Follow Me..., and I will make you fishers of Men." Immediately they left their nets and followed him [becoming His disciples, believing and trusting in Him and following His example].

I could never understand why men would do this, but I understand very well now!

The next one was in chapter 5, and those were the "B" attitudes.

Matthew 5:3–12 (AMP):

"Blessed [spiritually prosperous, happy, to be admired] are the poor in spirit [those devoid of spiritual arrogance, those who regard themselves as insignificant], for theirs is the kingdom of heaven [both now and forever].

"Blessed [forgiven, refreshed by God's Grace] and those who mourn [over their sins and repent], for they will be comforted [when the burden of sin is lifted].

"Blessed [inwardly peaceful, spiritually secure, worthy of respect] are the gentle [the kind-hearted, the sweet-spirited, the self-controlled], for they will inherit the earth.

"Blessed [joyful, nourished by God's goodness] are those who hunger and thirst for righteousness [those who actively seek right standing with God], for they will be [completely] satisfied.

"Blessed [content, sheltered by God's promises] are the merciful, for they will receive mercy.

"Blessed [anticipating God's presence spiritually mature] are the pure in heart [those with integrity, and courage and godly character], for they will see God.

Blessed [spiritually calm with life-joy in God's love] are the makers and maintainers of peace, for they will [express His character and] be called the sons of God.

"Blessed [comforted by inner peace and God's love] are those who are persecuted for doing that which is morally right, for theirs is the kingdom of heaven [both now and forever].

"Blessed [morally courageous and spiritually alive with life-joy in God's goodness] are you when people insult you and persecute you, and falsely say all kinds of evil things against you because of [your association with] Me. Be glad and exceedingly joyful for your reward in heaven is great [absolutely inexhaustible]; for in this same way they persecuted the prophets who were before you."

This was a joy just going back and reviewing the "B" attitudes. If one could live by them, it would be what the Lord wants for all of us.

Matthew 5:21–25 (AMP):

You have heard that it was said to the men of old "you shall not murder" and "whoever murders shall be guilty before the court." But I say to you that everyone who continues to be angry with his brother or harbors malice against him shall be guilty before the court; and whoever speaks [contemptuously and insultingly] to his brother, "Raca (you empty headed idiot)!" shall be guilty before the supreme court (Sanhedrin); and whoever says "You fool!" shall be in danger of the fiery hell. So if you are presenting your offering at the altar, and while there you remember that your brother has something [such as a grievance or legitimate complaint] against you, leave your offering there at the altar and go. First make peace with your brother and then come and present your offering. Come to terms quickly [at the earliest opportunity] with your opponent at law while you are with him on the way [to court]...

This was a radical difference from what the people were used to at the time.

Matthew 5:43 (TLB), "There is a saying, 'Love your friends and hate your enemies.' But I say: Love your enemies! Pray for those who persecute you!"

Matthew 6:1 (TLB), "Take care! Don't do your good deeds publicly, to be admired, for then you will lose the reward from your Father in heaven."

Matthew 6:9 (TLB), "Our Father in heaven, we honor your holy name."

Matthew 7:1 (TLB), "Don't criticize and you won't be criticized!"

Matthew 7:26 (TLB), "But those who ignore my instructions are foolish, like a man who builds his house on sand."

Matthew 9:13 (AMP):

> Go and learn what this [Scripture] means: "I DESIRE COMPASSION [for those in distress] AND NOT [animal] SACRIFICE," for I did not come to call [to repentance] the [self-proclaimed] righteous [who see no need to change], but sinners [those who recognize their sin and actively seek forgiveness].

Mark 11:24–26 (AMP):

> For this reason I am telling you, whatever things you ask for in prayer [in accordance with God's will], believe [with confident trust] that you have received them, and they will be given to you. Whenever you stand

praying, if you have anything against anyone, forgive him [drop the issue, let it go], so that you Father who is in heaven will also forgive you your transgressions and wrongdoings [against Him and others]. [But if you do not forgive, neither will your Father in heaven forgive your transgressions].

Key word: "forgive."

Powerful people hold grudges and pray, and prayers are not answered. They want to know why when they are holding a grudge against somebody. It doesn't work that way. You must forgive then ask; you cannot hold a grudge and go to God and ask for anything. It also must be consistent with His Word.

Isaiah 54:17 (KJV), "No weapon that is formed against thee shall prosper; and every tongue that shall rise against thee in judgment thou shalt condemn. This is the heritage of the servants of the LORD, and their righteousness is of me, saith the LORD."

The Lord will protect us from those who attack us. I repeat this scripture many times. It is comforting to know that. We have tools to protect us.

Luke 19:22 (KJV), "And he saith unto him, Out of thine mouth I will judge thee, evil servant: thou knewest that I was an austere man, taking up what I did not lay down, and reaping what I did not sow!"

I have used this scripture with my children, telling them whatever they put into something, that's what they are going to get out. Especially with schoolwork. If you do the work, you will get the grades. If you work at anything with the spirit of the Lord, you will reap the best.

Second Corinthians 5:8 (KJV), "We are confident, I say, and willing rather absent from the body and to be present with the Lord."

This is a scripture I used with my children to explain to them, "Mother died, but she is absent from the body and present with the Lord." It was some consolation. Although they had lost their mother, they knew she was with the Lord.

Psalm 3:3 (KJV), "But thou, O Lord, art a shield for me: My glory and the lifter up of mine head."

When I found myself in trouble, I used this scripture, and I could feel the love of God around me. I used this many times in my life. "Thou, O Lord, art a shield for me."

Isaiah 40:31 (KJV), "But they that wait upon the LORD shall renew their strength; they shall mount up with wings as eagles' they shall run and not be weary; and they shall walk, and not faint."

This is a good scripture to teach patience. If you wait upon the Lord, He will renew your strength. This is something I have to remind myself many times.

Sometimes, I run ahead of the Lord, or I get impatient waiting for an answer to prayer.

Psalm 23 (KJV):

> The Lord is my shepherd: I shall not want.
> He maketh me to lie down in green pastures:
> He leadeth me beside the still waters.
> He restoreth my soul:
> He leadeth me in the paths of righteousness
> for his name's sake.
> Yea, though I walk through the valley of the
> shadow of death I will fear no evil
> For thou art with me. Thy rod and thy staff
> they comfort me.
> Thou preparest a table before me in the
> presence of mine enemies:
> Thou anointest my head with oil, my cup
> runneth over.
> Surely goodness and mercy shall follow me all
> the days of my life:
> And I will dwell in the house of the Lord
> forever.

This scripture has a place in my heart and in the heart of my wife. She told me that, as a little girl, she went to the church across the street from where she lived and read a Bible in that church and read this scripture. This was also read at her celebration. I could remember the teacher in fifth grade in Jersey City reading Psalm 23 every morning. That's what all teachers did at that time. The year was 1947; how times have changed.

Psalm 34 (KJV), a psalm of David when he changed his behavior before Abimelech, who drove him away, and he departed.

> I will bless the Lord at all times:
> His praise shall continually be in my mouth.
> My soul shall make her boast in the LORD:
> The humble shall hear thereof, and be glad.
> O magnify the Lord with me,
> And let us exalt his name together.
> I sought the Lord and he heard me,
> And delivered me from all my fears.
> They looked unto him, and were lightened:
> And their faces were not ashamed.
> This poor man cried, and the Lord heard him,
> And saved him out of all his troubles.
> The angel of the Lord encampeth round about
> them that fear him,
> And delivered them.
> O taste and see the Lord is good:
> Blessed is the man that trusteth in him.

This psalm is put into a song sung by the Brooklyn Tabernacle Choir, and it is just beautiful. The important point is I sought the Lord, and He heard me and delivered me from my fears. And when He says, "Taste and see the Lord is good," to me, He is saying, "Try the Lord, and you will be blessed."

Acts 2:4 (KJV), "And they were all filled with the Holy Ghost and began to speak with other tongues as the Spirit gave them utterance."

The church I was at defined "tongue" as being the language of the Holy Spirit, and in my time, a prophecy would follow such an utterance.

Acts 2:17 (KJV):

And it shall come to pass in the last days, saith God,
I will pour out my Spirit upon all flesh:
And your sons and your daughters shall prophesy,
And your young men shall see visions,
And your old men shall dream dreams.

Joseph's Dream

I would like to finish this chapter with the story of Joseph and his dream. Joseph was a person who had the favor of God in his life and was the one who was more like Jesus in the Old Testament. His brothers were very jealous of him. One of the reasons was his father bought him a beautiful colorful robe, and the brothers did not like that. Joseph told the brother of a dream that he had that they (the brothers) were going to bow down to him later in life. They resented his attitude, and when they got a chance, the brothers threw him in a well. When merchants came, the brother sold him to the merchants who were on their way to Egypt. The other brother dipped the robe in goat's blood and took it back to the father and told him that Joseph was killed. The father mourned the death of his son for many weeks.

In Egypt, Joseph was a slave for Potiphar, and he earned his favor. Potiphar put him in charge of all that he owned. Potiphar's wife told a story about Joseph to Potiphar, and Potiphar put Joseph in jail. Joseph had a reputation for interpreting dreams, so Potiphar sent for him, and he interpreted that dream for him.

Joseph told Potiphar about a famine that would be coming, and Potiphar wanted to know what to do, so Joseph told him to store up food for the famine. People came from other countries to buy food from Potiphar, and the brothers showed up in Egypt. When Joseph told the brothers who he was, they were afraid; he told them not to be and that if he did not come to Egypt, he could not help them and their father.

Joseph had favor from God to do what he did, but he also had forgiveness and was a man with humility. He had a love for God, or God would not have blessed him like He did. It is my belief that the God who came to

Joseph is the same God that came to me and can come to anybody if they recognize Him with a strong love and have humility. God will work in your life. One other thing you have to look for is if you don't look with faith, you won't see His love and favor.

CHAPTER ELEVEN

The Last Chapter

I call this "The Last Chapter" because it is the last chapter in the book, but it is not the last chapter in my life. When you see all the grace God has given me, you might say to yourself, "Yes, but what is happening now?" I'm going to try to explain what is happening now and what is going to happen in the future.

Irene was sick from 2005 to 2017, and she had two bouts with cancer from which she was healed. The biggest problem she had was emphysema. When she went home to be with the Lord, I went through a tough period. We were married for fifty-nine years, and I took care of her for a long period of time. When she went home, I now did not have a wife, and I did not have anybody to take care of. This was a big adjustment. My golf partners, Frank and Tom, kind of kept me busy and made sure I did not feel sorry for myself. I decided that I had to move and put the house up for sale. My brother George is a broker, so we listed the house, and I thought it would sell right away. It was over a year before it was sold. I remember praying and asking God what I was doing wrong that nobody was even looking at my house. I had to make a big decision, and that was I had to change realtors. I did change, and still no potential buyers. I can remember like it was yesterday sitting in my bedroom and talking to God and saying to Him, "What do I have to do to get this house sold?" I did not hear a word, but in my mind, I heard, "Add another room." This house was a two-bedroom that was 2800 square feet. There was a way to take part of the bedroom that I had for an office and make another room. I told my brother that he could sell me the next house, and he was happy with that. So I was the contractor, and I hired people to come in and do the work. The main worker was a boy my brother had on his soccer team, and he did a great job. The room looked beautiful with a vinyl floor that looked like wood.

To make a long story short, when it was finished, I had three bids on the house and got the price I wanted. I know that was God's favor.

The next step was to look for a home. I looked in the senior citizen community in Toms River. We looked at many homes that were for sale at the time, and I was not happy with any of the homes. One day when we were out just about to go home, Marian, George's wife, said, "What about the house on Troumaka Street?" We were supposed to go see that home and never made it.

We looked at the house. George had the lockbox key, so we went in and looked around, and this house was different. It had a back sunroom that had baseboard heat and fifteen Andersen windows. I told George, "This is the house; make a bid on this house." I got the house for about $160,000.

I remodeled it with me doing most of the work, and I just refinanced this home, and the appraisal came in at $320,000. The mortgage guy could not believe it, but that's what it is worth right now. I doubled in price in two and a half years. I have never heard of such a thing, but I am very happy. My friends, that is the favor of God on my life. I had bought a house for $160,000, and now it's worth $320,000.00 in two and a half years; unbelievable. The only thing I know is anything is possible with God through faith.

I have another little story I would like to conclude with. Do you remember the boy who called me and told me, "We tried everything. Why don't we try God?" when we wanted to get into college? Just keep that in mind when I tell you the other story.

I got a call from a friend of mine's wife. Her husband died about thirty years ago. We wrote back and forth, and finally, I said, "Why don't we have lunch in Jersey City, where we both are from? It would be a good way to establish old relations."

We decided that we would go to the Hamilton Inn in downtown Jersey City, which looks like New York City. Just an aside, this was not too far from where my grandparents lived many years ago. We decided to meet at 12:30 p.m., so the place and time were set. I decided to leave a little early because I was traveling from Toms River, and it's about one hour and fifteen minutes to Jersey City. When I got there, I did not know where to park. My daughter Karen taught in a school right near there. She told me the police gave out tickets very freely in that area. So I pulled up to Hamilton Park, and I asked a man who had on an orange jacket where I could park. He told me, and I parked. I walked across the street, and I saw the same man in front of these big doors that looked like a church. So I asked the man again if it was all right to go in. He said, "Sure, I'm going in," so we both went in. It was a church, and there was a mass, so I stayed for the mass. There were about five people in this massive church. I felt bad for the priest. I knew the collection was not much, so I gave him something for the poor box.

As I was standing outside talking to the priest, he told me that the church had the shrine of St. Jude, and this was the shrine that brought George and me downtown sixty-five years ago. I had never gone back to that church in all those years. Now I was getting excited, and this was a confirmation from the Lord. Just a little smile from Him to say, "Good and faithful servant."

At this point, I hadn't seen Pat yet. So I went to the restaurant, and she was not there, so I went back to tell the priest, and everything was locked.

I hadn't seen her in years, and she did not know I was a Christian and that I was writing a book about the favor in my life. I had a lot of explaining to do, and she was understanding to a degree.

It was almost like a good movie. The restaurant called the Hamilton Inn in downtown Jersey City was nice. A beautiful day with two old friends meeting in the city where they both grew up and now meeting for lunch after not seeing each other for about sixty years. She still looked great, and the conversation was also great. The setting was Jersey City, but you would think that you were in New York and the buildings spilled over into Jersey City. Now I had a happening; I visited the church that started the adventure in my life. There were so many things that happened to me in the sixty-five years I could not update Pat with all that happened in my life. To me, this (finding this church like I did) was a confirmation about this book that I am writing and the fact that He told me to write this book. I was not thrilled at the time because I had papers and reports to do all my life. The more I thought about it, the more it started to sink in. The God of this world wanted me to represent Him by writing a story about my life and how it could help other people. What an honor that He should choose me for this project. I am perfect; no, I am a sinner. Yes, saved by Grace.

On the way home, I called Father Bob. He gave me the program of masses for the church; I had his phone number.

I explained the story to him, and he told me I made his day. He would like to see the book when I finish it, and I told him if he wanted me to give my testimony in his church, I would.

I will try to bring it all together about how I feel about favor or grace in my life. I was a young boy, and my father died, but I now realize that God is the Father of us all. It is my belief that He gave me favor at a young age. He put people in my life to help guide me and help me along the way. They were teachers, football coaches, and fellow students.

Another milestone in my life was when George Tardif called me and said to me, "We tried everything else. Why don't we try God?" That turn to God was one of the keys to my life. God wants us to turn to Him, and He wants to help us. All we have to do is to recognize Him and come to Him in humility, and He will be there. The following year we both had scholarships and played college football.

Another milestone was when I met my wife of fifty-nine years. I did not have a job; I did not have any money; all I had was the clothing on my back. He helped me to get married with a beautiful wedding and finish my degree. After graduation, I had a job within the two weeks that I was home. I got my dream job; I was a football coach.

Another time, He blessed me with two children. My two girls were born when I was working in Jersey City. I was also blessed with a good wife who cared for me and took good care of me.

He also blessed me with good friends. When I make a friend, I love them for life. Ralph was my best friend, and he was put in my life as a bother; he helped me, and I helped him. I miss him. He died soon after my wife died. Jim Taylor, my roommate, and I still see each other after sixty-five years. Sal and Dee Graziano, By the Grace of God team. These people were all a blessing to me, and I thank them from my heart. Later in life, Ted Guyuski and his wife, Maryanne, lived near us and went to our church from the '80s.

This project will end, and I will look for another project to do in service to the Lord. I will pray to the Lord that He helps me to find something He wants me to do. I am closing. In 1977, I opened my heart to Jesus, and He came in big time; that's when my ministry in my job happened. If you are reading this book and don't have Jesus in your heart, it is simple. Just ask Him to forgive your sins and come into your heart to be your Savior. John 3:16 (KJV) says, "For God so loved the world that he gave his only begotten son, that whosoever believeth in him should not perish, but have everlasting life."

What this says to me is that to have everlasting life, you have to believe in Him and accept Him. If you do, you will have everlasting life. Whoever trusts Jesus will have everlasting life. To trust someone, you have to know them, so you must develop a relationship with Him by believing in Him and asking Him to be your Savior in your heart.

Ending in the Holman School

The Holman staff was seeing me as a mature Christian. I think I had a little more understanding with this staff, and I was a little more open. All in all, it was a fantastic relationship. I was not in this state of mind for the other school, but I have a fond memory, plus it was the last school I was a principal of. I would like to conclude with an inscription they put on a plaque. I would like to thank all the teachers that I worked with over the thirty years in Jackson; people in the high school; Larry and Carol D'Zio, who are still friends; the staff at the Goetz Lynn Allen; the staff at the HC Johnson School. I would like to thank the staff at the Holman School; this was the last staff I worked with, and I want to thank them for the love they showed me in the last years in Jackson. I can't thank you enough.

Special thank you to my wife of fifty-nine years and the blessing of three children (Irene, Karen, and John) and five grandchildren, John Thomas Kounelias, Justin Kounelias, Jacob Russo, Faith Amabile, Ava Amabile.

This was a plaque given to me at my retirement dinner.

Second Timothy 4:7 (KJV), "I have fought a good fight. I have finished my course. I have kept the faith."

1964–1994. "Those were the days, my friend." (Jackson Schools)

The teachers at my retirement sang, "Those were the days, my friend; we thought they would never end."

I thank You, Lord, for a wonderful life with so many good people. You blessed me and gave me favor so that I could share my life with other people so You could help them like You have helped me.

Closure Takeaway

Isaiah 54:13 (ESV), "All your children shall be taught by the Lord, and great shall be the peace of your children."

My father died when I was twelve years old. I had many different feelings about what was going on in my life. My first reaction was sadness and thinking about what might happen to me. My second reaction was, *What can I do to help the situation?* The only thing I could think about was how much I loved my father and my mother. My father was gone, working out of state, so I only saw him on weekends; however, I had a very close relationship with my mother. My thoughts were, *Is there anything I can do to help this situation and help my mother?* I don't remember the sequence, but I know my mother went into a deep depression, and the family customs did not help. The women wore black for about a year and could not wear make-up or really go out. One other thing I remember was we could not listen to the radio. We did not have a TV at the time, or that would have been out. So not only did you lose someone, but now you also had to live in a very dark environment. My mother was not this kind of a person. She was outgoing and fun to be around. Now because of a tradition, it made it worse.

By researching Scripture, it is plain to see that God wanted the best for little children. He plainly wanted to teach little children and write on their hearts the way they should go. I was introduced to the priest at Our Lady of Mount Carmel Church, and this gave me insight on what God wanted from me. It is my contention that when my father died, I wanted to please God, learning from the teachings at the church.

The takeaway here is God never leaves you or forsakes you, especially little children. All your children will be taught by God, but as adults, we must set the stage and get them to the right place. I cringe when I see some of the decisions that parents are making for their children. I thank God for my uncle, who stepped up and took me to church when my father died and introduced me to the priest. This was monumental, and I did not realize that for a long time. What we did as a family was turn to God in a time of need, especially as a family without a father. For whatever reason, my uncle stepped in. It might be because I was at a young age living in the city, and he wanted to keep me out of trouble. I believe the Lord, as said in the Scripture, "All children shall be taught by the Lord."

"Takeaway"

When your family is in trouble, seek the Lord.

I felt a need to help my mother financially, but what could a twelve-year-old boy do? Paper route, shine shoes, which helped a little. My mother was a very loving person who you just wanted to help. I did by trying to fix the house we bought, and I was not that good at that, but I tried really hard.

When it came time for me to go to college, some family members thought I should stay home and help my widowed mother. My mother stopped that move and said If I could go to college, that's what I should do, and she would be all right with that. Thank God she had the insight and encouraged me.

Proverbs 22:6 (KJV), "Train up a child in the way he should go; even when he is old, he will not depart from it."

BY THE GRACE OF GOD

Ephesians 6:4 (ESV), "Fathers do not provoke your children to anger but bring them up in the discipline and instructions of the Lord."

Psalm 127:3 (AMP), "Behold, children are a heritage from the Lord, the fruit of the womb a reward."

Romans 8:14 (ESV), "For all who are led by the spirit of God are sons of God."

Matthew 19:14 (ESV), "But Jesus said, 'Let the little children come to me and do not hinder them, for to such belongs the kingdom of heaven.'"

Second Corinthians 6:18 (ESV), "And I will be a father to you and you shall be sons and daughters to me, says the Lord Almighty."

God Loves the World

John 3:16 (KJV), "For God so loved the world...that whosoever believeth in him should not perish, but have everlasting life."

This is a key scripture talking about God and His Son. He gives us the way to everlasting life. God so loved the world that He gave His Son to show life after death but also the love He has for His people. If you were to ask me what scripture would be more important than another, I would put this one in that category. The reason is that it is the backbone to Christianity. Christ came to die for our sins as a living sacrifice and rose on the third day to show us all the way. John explains that God sent His Son to earth as a man to bear our sins so that we didn't have sin by accepting Jesus as our Savior. Whoever believes in Jesus will have "eternal life" and experience some of His blessings in this lifetime.

My testimony is an example of what happens when you accept Jesus in your life and listen to what He is telling you and what way or what dream you should pursue.

I have tried to follow what my heart told me and the little nudging in my gut, but there were times when I have misread, and I looked for doors that were open and closed and proceeded through the open door. As I got older, I got the message, and I knew when He was speaking to me and what He wanted from me. If your dreams are in line with the Word of God, things seem to go a little easier.

I went through a soul-searching activity when I decided to write this book. It kept coming up in my mind, and I thought maybe He was saying "a legacy." So I started out with a legacy, and I showed it to a few people, and they said, "I think you have a book, not a legacy." So I got in prayer, and it was clear that He wanted me to write a book. So I said, "I have been doing papers and reports throughout my career. I'm tired." A voice inside me said, "Are you happy for what I did for you?" When you come to think of it, how could I say no? God wanted to use my life to influence somebody. When

I thought about it, I was thrilled! So I contacted TBN, and they wanted some samples of my writing, so I sent them two chapters. In about three weeks, they came back with a yes. At first, I could not believe it, but now I had the green light, and I knew that was a confirmation for the book.

Faith

Second Timothy 3:15 (KJV), "And that from a child thou hast known the holy scriptures, which are able to make thee wise unto salvation through faith which is in Christ Jesus."

My friend George did not know about my background in the church when I was young and in grammar school. But he called me as if I would respond the way I did. I knew all about Jesus, but I did not know Jesus. We both had faith that if we called on God, something might happen. Our faith was weak at this time in life, but we continued to go to this church for about six weeks before the friend called George and told him that he would like to see him, and he eventually played football in that school and graduated from St. Benedict's. For me, it was a little different. I waited longer, and George called me in the spring of that year. I know I did not go to that church all year. We were not aware of scripture that said, "But the scripture hath concluded all under sin, that the promise by faith of Jesus Christ might be given to them that believe" (Galatians 3:22, KJV).

Now I understand, but all I thought of at the time was the Lord came through for us, and we were very happy. This became a problem for those in my family who did not understand. They were saying, "How can you get a scholarship from somebody that you don't even know or have ever seen?" This message was so strong in my spirit that I would not listen to anybody; I just knew I had to go. As I look back, I apply the lights again. As long as the light was green, I would proceed until I got stopped, and that never happened. This faith walk was the start of a wonderful career. I just think I would never have been given the opportunity to write this book about what happened in my life without the blessings of the Lord.

The faith I had then is still the faith that I have now. I don't know if this book is for one person or 500 people, but it is well worth it if it only helps one person.

Favor

Another important part of my testimony is the favor of God. I believe when I humbly looked for God, He touched my life. It should not get confused with favoritism; you get favor when you humbly recognize Him. Make Him your focus of everyday life. Do things that please God, and you have the key. If you look through Scripture, the people who had favor with God were pleasing to Him. Therefore, if you want favor with God, do things that please Him.

When you have favor with God, that does not mean everything is rosy; you will still have the problems of regular life, but now you have much hope in your life that you will be able to solve many of your problems with His help. Mel Walker defines "favor" as "divine kindness or true compassion on the part of God Himself toward needy and undeserving human recipients." Often in Scripture, this act of God toward unworthy men or women is referred to as "God's grace," which means "the unmerited favor of God," as Justin Holcomb said on Christianity.com.

I would like to share ten keys to obtaining the favor of God written by Ward Simpson on October 9, 2018.

Ward Simson has an introduction that I think is important: "Favor is not love, God loves everyone the same. It's not grace, we are saved through grace by faith. It's also not about blessing although God's favor leads to blessing. Favor is something more and it will change your life."

Ten Keys to God's Favor by Ward Simpson
    1.   Love God

Love God with all your heart. Without loving Him, we cannot expect to gain His favor.

> My son do not forget My teaching, but keep my commands in your heart, for they will prolong your life many years and being your peace and prosperity. Let love and faithfulness never leave you, bind them around your...heart. Then you will win favor and a good name in the sight of God and man.
>
> Proverbs 3:1–4 (NIV)

2.   Love people

What are you doing for the kingdom? What are you doing for others? If you want God's favor, then start caring for people. Ruth found favor with Boaz because of the things she had done, and James says, "Faith without works is dead."

"The King will reply, 'Truly I tell you, whatever you did for one of the least of these brothers and sisters of mine, you did for me'" (Matthew 25:40, NIV).

> Boaz replied, "I've been told all about what you have done for your mother-in-law since the death of your husband—how you left your father and mother and your homeland and came to live with a people you did not know before. May the Lord repay you for what you have done. May you be rightly rewarded by the Lord, the God of Israel, under whose wings you have come to take refuge."

Ruth 2:11–12 (NIV)

Ruth was noticed for what she had done. She received more than she asked for, special treatment, protection, more than enough.

3. Hate what God hates

As you make a stand for God and His cause, His favor is released upon you.

"But you have this in your favor: You hate the practices of Nicolaitans, which I also hate" (Revelation 2:6, NIV).

4. Give gifts and offerings

Abel's offering found favor with God, but Cain's did not. Make sure your offering finds favor with God. Giving gifts leads us to find favor with both God and man, as we see from the example of Jacob, who found favor with Esau following his substantial gift.

5. Be faithful

Noah found favor with God due to his faithfulness. He walked faithfully with God, and that led to favor.

> So the Lord said, "I will wipe from the face of the earth the human race I have related and with them the animals, the birds and creatures that move along the ground—for

I regret that I have made them." But Noah found favor in the eyes of the Lord. This is the account of Noah and his family. Noah was a righteous man, blameless among the people of his time and he walked faithfully with God.

Genesis 6:7–9 (NIV)

6. Be righteous/blameless

As we can also see in the example of Noah, being righteous and blameless is a key to finding favor. We also find this call to righteousness in the New Testament.

"...seek first the Kingdom of God and His righteousness and all these things will be added unto you" (Matthew 6:33, ESV).

"Surely, Lord, you bless the righteous, you surround them with your favor as a shield" (Psalm 5:12, NIV). You can be blessed with favor; favor leads to blessings.

7. Submitted

Esther shows us how submission brings favor. She didn't take matters into her own hands. This is an ingredient to reviving favor. She exemplified submission, humility, and confidence in God and won the favor of everyone who saw her.

"When the turn came for Esther...to go to the king, she asked for nothing other than what Hegai, the king's eunuch who was in charge of the harem, suggested" (Esther 2:15, NIV).

8.   Be humble/have humility

Through her humility, Esther received immediate care and attention, provision, the best place, helpers, assistants, and attendants. Furthermore, her favor created favor for all around her. Through our humility, let's create an atmosphere of favor in our lives that can overflow to others.

"God resists the proud, but gives grace to the humble" (1 Peter 5:5, NKJV).

9.   Be honest

Honest is a key to favor. Joseph found favor with Potiphar because he could be trusted.

"The Lord detests dishonest scales, but accurate weights find favor with him" (Proverbs 11:1, NIV).

"Joseph found favor in his eyes and became his attendant. Potiphar put him in charge of his household and entrusted in his care everything he owned" (Genesis 39:4, NIV).

10.   Wisdom

Wisdom is a key to favor. As Solomon makes clear in the book of Proverbs, "For those who find me find life and receive favor from the Lord" (Proverbs 8:35, NIV).

God's favor is lasting, "For His anger lasts only a moment but his favor lasts a lifetime..." (Psalm 30:5, NIV).

Weeping may stay for the night, but rejoicing comes in the morning.

Once you have God's favor, it lasts a lifetime.

Do you want a lifetime of favor? Use these ten keys to unlock God's increased provision in your life and let it overflow to others.

Noah found favor; he was blameless, righteous, and faithful. Joseph found favor with God, as did Esther. God's favor is for a purpose. When He favors you, it's not to sit upon but to do something with. You receive blessing so you can be a blessing.

Love Takeaway

It can be said that God is love. It can be explained as wanting the best for another person. God's love is for everyone, and He wants the best for each one of us. The only thing that we have to do is recognize Him and give Him the glory and worship that He wants from us. He has the highest degree of love anybody can give you. He sent His Son to die for us as a living sacrifice for our sins, and we can live through Him.

Paul defined love in 1 Corinthians 13 (NIV). It is looked upon by scholars as the best definition of love.

> Love is patient, love is kind. It does not envy, it does not boast, it is not proud. It does not dishonor others, it is not self-seeking, it is not easily angered, it keeps no record of wrongs.

Love does not delight in evil but rejoices with the truth. It always protects, always trusts, always hopes, always preserves.

Love never fails. But where there are prophecies, they will cease; where there are tongues, they will be stilled; where their knowledge, it will pass away. For we know in part and we prophesy in part, but when completeness comes, what is in part disappears. When I was a child, I talked like a child, I thought like a child, I reasoned like a child. When I become a man, I put the ways of childhood behind me. For now we see only a reflection as in a mirror; then we shall see face to face. Now I know in part; then I shall know fully even as I am fully known.

And now these three remain: faith, hope, and love. But the greatest of these is love.

There is another part of love in the Bible, and that is the "agape" kind of love. The only way I can explain it from the research that I did is it is another level; it is accepting Jesus, the Son of God, in your life. When you accept Jesus in your heart, you look at all the parts in 1 Corinthians 13 and add the love of God, and you have the whole thing.

Agape kind of love is the God level of love. When I accepted Jesus into my heart, my wife did the same thing, so we were both born again. She had God's love in her heart, and so did I. We were married for fifty-nine years, and this was the best love we had for each other. There is no way I could explain my love for her at this time; I can only say it was something we did not have up to that point in our marriage.

This is a very important "takeaway." Men, accept Jesus into your heart, and women, do the same and see what happens to your marriage.

If you both are born again, renew your vows with an agape (God kind of love).

CPSIA information can be obtained
at www.ICGtesting.com
Printed in the USA
BVHW030318160822
644635BV00006B/53